Paris and Parisians

The Cheapo Snob Explores the City and Its Famous French Residents

Jayne R. Boisvert

Published by Open Books

Copyright © 2021 by Jayne R. Boisvert

Cover images ©KIRAYONAK YULIYA shutterstock.com/g/
KIRAYONAK+YULIYA

©Olga_C shutterstock.com/g/Olga_C

Interior design by Siva Ram Maganti

ISBN-13: 978-1948598439

For Alex and Daniel—my two sons who make me proud

CONTENTS

Preface

CHEAPO SNOBS ABOUND, IT seems. Nearly everyone I meet shares my travel philosophy: the desire to maintain high standards while keeping spending to a minimum. If you hold similar views and love the city of Paris, this might be just the guidebook to fill the bill. While reading the following pages, the Cheapo side of you will relish the many free and low-cost options while your inner Snob will enjoy splurges to satisfy your craving for luxury. One problem, as I see it, is that not all of us are cut from the same cloth. A certain Cheapo Snob, for example, might want to save on rooms and entrance fees to attractions while preferring to pay more for meals. Another's tastes might be quite the opposite. Over the course of this book, I hope to remedy this dilemma.

The first two chapters will allow travelers to determine exactly where they stand on the Cheapo-Snob spectrum when it comes to lodging and dining. Suggestions for accommodations begin with the low-cost winner "couchsurfing" and end up at palatial five-star hotels. Now there's a range for you! The same holds true in the dining category. Real budget-minded visitors can pick up a falafel or a gyro for lunch or dinner, or choose to stop in at a fast-food joint or an inexpensive *bouillon*. If you decide that eating out is your preferred way of pleasing the Snob in you (and money is no object), dinner at the Jules Verne on the Eiffel Tower or in some of the restaurants frequented by American celebrities might be worth the exorbitant prices. The choice is yours. The third chapter of this guide, which focuses on twelve popular attractions in and near the City of Light, provides the history of the sites as well as a list of current entry fees.

Cheapos might be strongly attracted to the free offerings: a tour of Saint-Sulpice church, for example, or a visit to the home of Balzac or Hugo. On the other hand, frugal visitors may balk at having to pay twenty-one euros to get into the Marmottan Monet museum. It's all a matter of your priorities. One word of warning: you won't find well-known sites like the Louvre, Notre-Dame, or the Eiffel Tower included here. For those and other similar venues, check out my previous Cheapo Snob book: *Pilgrimage to Paris*.

In Chapters 4 through 13 we look at a wide variety of renowned French people who at one time chose to make Paris their home. You'll find an alphabetical listing of nineteenth – and twentieth-century actors, architects, artists, authors, chefs, fashion designers, photographers, politicians, and a few others who don't fit into those categories. Many of their names will be quite familiar: Bardot, Eiffel, Monet, Piaf, and Pasteur...just to give you an idea. Others such as Nadia Boulanger, Paul Poiret, and Louis Blériot may be new to you but may prove to be equally fascinating. For the nominal cost of a bus or métro ticket Cheapos will enjoy exploring new areas associated with these prominent figures. And Snobs might want to visit some of their heroes' favorite hangouts. So, who won't you find in these sections? Well, Americans for one and people who were born in countries other than France—with the exception of Algeria which was a French colony until 1962. Hemingway, Stein, Fitzgerald, and company don't make the cut (they're also in *Pilgrimage to Paris*), nor will the Curies, Yves Montand, Simone Signoret, or Van Gogh... who just have to wait for volume three of the Cheapo Snob series.

Chapter 1

Lodging

THE NUMBER OF ACCOMMODATIONS in the City of Light is nothing short of astounding. This means that the search for a place to stay can be quite an ordeal. Taking into account only hotels with a star rating (based on one to five stars), there are over 2,000 choices available. Never fear! We're here to help you sort things out. Before beginning, however, Snobs as well as Cheapos should consider renting an apartment from a reputable source such as Vrbo, HomeAway, or Airbnb. The wide variety of sizes and prices of this type of lodging should accommodate almost any family and budget. But first, here are some key questions to consider.

- How many square meters are there? Being stuck in an overly small dwelling might prove uncomfortable; by way of comparison, an American hotel room averages twenty-five to thirty square meters.

- What floor is the apartment located on? Remember what we call the second floor is their first... and so on.

- Is there an elevator in the building? You probably don't want to be climbing up to the *3ème étage* (fourth floor) loaded down with heavy bags or groceries. Even if there is an elevator, it's usually quite small, so remember to pack as light as you can before leaving home.

- Which arrondissement is it located in? To best suit your travel needs you might not want to be out in the 17ᵗʰ or 20ᵗʰ, for example.

- Besides apartment rental services like Vrbo, a more elegant option for Snobs is to book a rental through Paris Perfect which has lodgings mainly in the $200-plus per night range. Remember that prices can vary—mostly in an upward direction—from year to year.

For Cheapos

Like nearly all big cities worldwide, Paris can be a difficult place to find affordable lodging. Other than flights, housing usually represents the biggest expenditure of your trip. That being said, the extremely frugal-minded—mainly young and adventurous types—might consider "couchsurfing" or hostels as a way to stay within their budget. In this section we'll examine those two possibilities as well as some French budget chains and one – to three-star hotels. On the whole, the suggestions which follow fall into the $200 per night and under category. Cheapos should keep in mind that many Parisian hotel rooms, bathrooms, and especially shower stalls are much smaller than Americans would typically expect. As a result, they can often present quite a challenge to navigate.

- Couchsurfing, the Cheapo winner: As the name implies, this involves staying on someone's couch…or if you're in luck, in the spare bedroom depending on the circumstances. After paying a small membership fee (fifteen dollars/year at this point), you'd only need to bring a small gift or cook a meal for the host. No money for the lodging is ever exchanged.

- For the young (or the young at heart): Hostel accommodations—from as low as twenty-five dollars to fifty dollars per night—are hard to beat. Most offer dorms with shared bathrooms although some private rooms with private baths are available. Sheets are provided but you may need to bring or rent towels. Some top-rated hostels include:

    o Saint Christopher's Inn Gare du Nord and Generator Paris (both in the 10ᵗʰ)

- Les Piaules (11th) which is a good choice for couples and families

  ○ Les Piaules (11th) which is a good choice for couples and families

  ○ Another Cheapo idea, consider contacting one of the apartment rental services listed previously such as Airbnb to book a room in someone's house

- In the one-star category: A website called Eurocheapo (you've got to love the name!) suggests a couple of popular hotels in the fifty-five dollars to seventy-five dollars range with clean, comfortable rooms. On a really tight budget—as long as you don't expect luxurious appointments and spacious quarters—one-stars might do. Also note that by law one-star French hotels are **not** required to employ staff members who speak foreign languages. A couple of possibilities:

  ○ Hôtel Tiquetonne (2nd)

  ○ Hôtel Marignan (5th)—not to be confused with the five-star of the same name on the Champs-Élysées

- Try a budget hotel:

  ○ Ibis, for example. With several branches throughout the capital including at Charles de Gaulle airport, these hotels offer clean but spartan rooms with absolutely no frills: two thin bath towels, a tiny shower stall and bathroom, and a relatively comfortable bed for about $130/night.

  ○ Timhotel also has diverse locations in the city with prices that vary according to their two – to four-star ratings. Figure on approximately $100-$180/night.

- Take a look at some two – or three-star hotels: These small hotels are clearly my favorite choice for getting a more-than-decent room in Paris. Please keep in mind that you might have to be willing to forgo "extras" such as elevators and air-conditioning. Here are a few dependable hotels all located in the 5th arrondissement:

  ○ In the two-star category, both the Vendôme Saint-Germain

and the Collège de France have doubles ranging from $145-180/night.

○ Three stars are required to be slightly more spacious than two stars. Rooms at the very well-located Hôtel Henri IV go for about $175/night. And the Hôtel des Grandes Écoles, which has a beautiful garden setting, has varying accommodations—from cramped to charming which are priced accordingly from $100-$180/night.

For Snobs

The words "Paris" and "luxury" go together—whether discussing the extravagance of the Louvre, the Opéra Garnier, or shops along the Champs-Élysées. The same is true for high-class accommodations. Despite certain caveats mentioned below, the City of Light exhibits its opulence in over 450 four-star hotels and nearly ninety five-stars. Recently an even higher designation, "palace," came into being. The world-famous Ritz naturally made that list. Its hotel and restaurants owe their name and reputation to the efforts of César Ritz and Auguste Escoffier during the Belle Époque at the turn of the twentieth century. (Check out Chef Escoffier in Chapter 8.) For his part, Ernest Hemingway once compared the Ritz to paradise: "When I dream of afterlife in heaven, the action always takes place in the Paris Ritz." Here are some of the top hotels the capital has to offer for your next stay…or simply for you to dream about.

First, a warning. The four-star category is kind of tricky since hotels can be specifically designed to meet the bare minimum criteria such as slightly larger rooms, elevators, air-conditioning, and breakfast service without being luxurious or even all that appealing. What this means is that there is a huge diversity in terms of prices and charm within the category. For example, the Novotel chain has a few four-star locations in the city, but the quality of their linens and starkness of the room décor are not much better than those found at the aforementioned Ibis…yet at a higher price. The same is true for Mercure hotels with a four-star rating. The beds may be comfy and many of the locations quite good, but overall the rooms might not be as impressive as you would imagine. However, if this Holiday Inn-type style is what you're looking for, these hotels could do nicely. Both Novotel and Mercure have rooms at $150-plus. Another proviso: some four-stars at decent prices are located in arrondissements off the beaten track, such as the Hôtel Ampère (17th). Not bad, really, as long as you're aware of the distance involved (and perhaps the need to take cabs or public transportation) before you commit.

A few tips:

- Find a "true" four-star hotel: A higher per night cost will undoubtedly provide you with the kind of luxury and charm you seek. Prices at the Hôtel Le Bourdonnais (7th), the Mansart (1st), and Hôtel Brighton (also in the 1st) extend from approximately $160 to $260 a night.

- Follow travelers' recommendations for five stars: Every year *Condé Nast Traveler* magazine puts out a list of its RCAs—Readers' Choice Awards. It should come as no surprise that their upscale readership would fall mainly into the "money is no object" category, meaning they choose a lot of the most expensive hotels available in Paris. So here are some of their 2019 selections which made it into the top fifteen, keeping in mind that they may be a notch below the even more chichi categories that follow: #5 Hôtel Esprit Saint Germain (6th), #8 Nolinski Paris (1st), #11 Hôtel Vernet (8th), #13 Hôtel du Collectionneur (8th), and #15 Saint James Paris (16th). Charm and luxury come with a high price tag. Figure on paying about $400-plus per night.

- Try a Gold List member: Editors at Condé Nast also publish their annual Gold List choices in the luxury category. Many repeat in the "palace" designation below so I'll just mention a few. The newly renovated Hôtel de Crillon (8th), established in 1758 on place de la Concorde, has the unique distinction that both Ben Franklin and Jacqueline Kennedy slept there. The Art Nouveau style Lutetia (6th) was one of the top picks along with the smaller boutique Hôtel Hoxton (2nd). All of the prices start from about $450 to $900 per night.

- Opt for a "palace" hotel: Since 2010 a new level of opulence was instituted to indicate institutions that go one better than five-stars by "contributing on a cultural level." More than ten hotels have received this distinction as of today. In the 1st arrondissement there's the Ritz Paris, Mandarin Oriental, and Hôtel Meurice (once a favorite of Salvador Dalí). The Shangri-La as well as the Peninsula Paris are both located in the 16th, the latter once frequented by George Gershwin back when it was called the Majestic. In the 2nd we find Park Hyatt Paris Vendôme. By far the greatest number of these "palaces" are found in the 8th arrondissement—Le Bristol, the Four Seasons George V, the Plaza Athénée, La Réserve Paris Hotel and Spa, and the Royal Monceau. Call me naïve but I had no idea that so many of these super luxury hotels existed, nor that prices could start at $600-plus per night and climb to $15,000 or more. Wow.

- Follow in Chanel's footsteps: For a mere $20,000 a night—which climbs to around $30,000 on holidays—you too can enjoy Coco Chanel's fabulous suite at the Ritz. Originally located at #302, all of her hand-selected furnishings were moved down one floor to room #202, providing guests with a better view of the place Vendôme. The suite is kind of a Chanel museum with lots of her personal items on view. Oh là là! (Read more about this famous fashion designer in Chapter 10.)

Chapter 2

Dining Options

PARIS, LIKE ALL BIG cities, offers a wide variety of dining experiences from the smallest bistro to the most elegant, three-star Michelin restaurant. However, there's a lot of flux in these establishments in terms of winning and losing stars as well as their actual existence. That being said, although some names and addresses will be provided, it is hoped that by reading through the following pages you'll be able to understand what's available so that you can navigate the world of dining on your own. In this chapter you'll find ideas to meet almost every taste and budget level. The Cheapo will be able to select from the lowliest fast-food joint, inexpensive (but tasty) food trucks, and ethnic selections as well as bistros and *bouillons*. For the Snob, the sky's the limit—both in terms of price and location, including the Jules Verne on level two of the Eiffel Tower and the Tour d'Argent on the seventh floor of its building across the Seine overlooking Notre-Dame. One word of warning: French restaurants have very strict hours of operation. Don't expect to waltz in almost anywhere, say, at 2:30 p.m. and expect to get lunch. Same goes for having supper before 7:00 p.m. or 7:30 p.m. Typical hours are from 12:00-2:30 p.m. and 7:30-11:00 p.m. So, here we go…off to examine dining in the City of Light.

For Cheapos

Even Cheapos will admit that, as a group, we're not all identical. The way we ate as twenty-year-olds may no longer be even vaguely on our radar screen decades later. So, although not all of these ideas will appeal to every frugal reader, here's a list of inexpensive dining options in more or less ascending order. By the way, as previously noted, it's a good idea to make sure the specified businesses are still in operation today. You never know.

- Grab a bite to eat at a supermarket: Monoprix, Carrefour, Franprix—you'll no doubt see these ubiquitous names as you stroll through the city. You can often pick up something like the old standby of cheese, ham or salami, and a baguette for a picnic by the Seine, on the Champ de Mars near the Eiffel Tower, or for eating in your room.

- Go to a *boulangerie*: Bakeries usually offer a pretty decent variety of quiches and sandwiches. Some might even have the French answer to the Italian focaccia bread, the *fougasse*. On a strict budget you might want to buy something during the afternoon for warming up in the microwave (if your room has one) at dinnertime.

- Check out *les fast-food*: Yes, they're all around—McDonald's, Burger King, Pizza Hut, KFC, not to mention the omnipresent Belgian hamburger chain Quick. Even if the food doesn't generally appeal to you, sometimes it's nice on a warm afternoon to drop in to McDo, as they call it, for a glass of beer and an order of fries.

- For a touch of class: If you're in the mood for something sweet, consider one of these two options. Frankly, there might be better pastry shops in Paris, but these enduring locations are legendary.

  o Angelina, 226, rue de Rivoli (1st)—this tea room, which has been around since 1903, serves pastries, luncheon items, as well as their famous African hot chocolate in a Belle Époque-type setting. To cut down on the price, consider getting take-out (*à emporter*); otherwise, it's best to reserve a table in advance.

- o Ladurée, a luxury bakery established in 1862, specializes in the *macaron* cookie, which is nothing like our American macaroon. There are several sites throughout the city including at 16, rue Royale (8th) and 21, rue Bonaparte (6th).

- Treat yourself to a crêpe: Both sweet (*crêpe*) and savory (*galette*) versions of the famous thin French pancakes are for sale from street vendors or, if you feel like going to a restaurant, there are plenty to choose from such as:

  - o Café Breizh, 109, rue Vieille du Temple (3rd)
  - o La Crêperie Josselin, 67, boulevard du Montparnasse (14th)

- Try the "best falafel in the world": Some of my all-time favorite sandwiches are the falafels found in the Marais (4th) at two locations a stone's throw from each other:

  - o L'As du Fallafel, 34, rue des Rosiers and
  - o Chez H'Anna up the street at #54

- How about a yummy gyro?: Check out these places all located in the 5th arrondissement.

  - o La Maison de Gyros 17, rue de la Huchette
  - o l'Île de Crête 10, rue Mouffetard
  - o Le Gyros 3, rue de la Harpe

- Look for a *traiteur*: A hard word to translate, sort of a mix between a butcher shop and a deli, these small shops offering a selection of precooked dishes are found nearly everywhere in the capital. Especially prominent are *traiteurs asiatiques* offering very tasty Chinese, Japanese, Thai, or Vietnamese specialties.

- Find a food truck: Paris has all sorts of meals on wheels which serve everything from Argentine empanadas to Pad Thai, ice cream, pizza, and bagels.

  - o Take a look at this website for more information: https://

www.france-hotel-guide.com/en/blog/food-trucks-paris/.

- o The very popular burger joint Le Camion qui Fume ("The Smoking Truck"), run by a California woman and her partner, can be found every day (except at lunchtime on Mondays) at MK2 Bibliothèque, 132, avenue de France (13th) from 12:00-2:30 p.m. and in the evening from 7:00-9:30 p.m. and on Tuesday and Friday 12:00-2:00 p.m. at 11, place de la Madeleine (8th). The couple has also recently opened a restaurant at 168, rue Montmartre (2nd).

- Consider a *bouillon*: Designed to provide nourishment for workers revamping the city in the late 1800s, some of these establishments have been serving up classic French cuisine at rock-bottom prices ever since. A word of warning: the Art Nouveau settings of many of them far outshine the quality of the meal according to many reviewers.

    - o Le Chartier at 7, rue du Faubourg Montmartre (9th), in operation since 1896, maintains unbeatable prices, but both the food and service have been described as mediocre. Its branch at 59, boulevard du Montparnasse (across from the train station in the 6th) has seen more favorable reviews for its atmosphere as well as its cuisine.

    - o Bouillon Julien, 16, rue du Faubourg Saint-Denis (10th), which has been around since 1906, is a meticulously restored historical landmark, and a one-time favorite of Édith Piaf. (Read about the famous *chanteuse* in Chapter 9.)

    - o Finally, if a first-rate meal matters much more to you than ambiance, try the newest bouillon, the modern Aca Pigalle at 48, boulevard de Clichy (18th). This spot is so well recognized as an excellent value that it pays to arrive during off hours or be prepared for a long wait to get inside.

- Go to a rooftop cafeteria: Several department stores in Paris have eating spaces on their top floors...which may not be exactly cheap but offer nice views of the city. Of course, to save a few euros you could just drop in for tea or coffee…or just to see and enjoy the panorama.

- o Le Bazar de l'Hôtel de Ville, called le BHV by the locals, located at 52, rue de Rivoli (4th) reveals parts of the surrounding Marais from its fifth-floor dining area

- o Printemps at 64, boulevard Haussmann (9th), which has amazing vistas of the city from its ninth-floor Déli-Cieux self-service, is accessed from the Beauté/Maison section of the store

- o Galeries Lafayette's options include a terrace on the seventh floor at 40, boulevard Haussmann and another on the sixth floor of the Lafayette Café, 27, rue de la Chaussée d'Antin

- Have a *plat du jour*: The "dish of the day," often posted outside a café on a chalkboard *(une ardoise)*, is a special meal offered at a very reasonable price. In general, having your big meal in the middle of the day is the absolute best way to save a few euros and keep to your budget.

- Look for "seals of approval:" *Le Guide du Routard, Le Petit Fûté, Gault Millau* and other French guidebooks endorse their favorite restaurants around the city by giving them *étiquettes* ("labels") to affix to their doors or windows. Some of the eateries—many of them bistros—are on the cheaper side. We've had a lot of luck by following these recommendations. Just be sure the year's date on the label is current. Another possibility is to check out restaurants in the arrondissement you're interested in via The Fork, a Trip Advisor company at https://www.thefork.com/restaurants/paris-c415144.

- If you're in the mood for a splurge: Try out some of the upscale bistros serving hearty traditional dishes.

- o The delightfully modern L'Assiette found at 181, rue du Château (14th)

- o The charming Petit Baigneur at 10, rue de la Sablière (also in the14th)

- o Le Petit Pontoise, 9, rue de Pontoise (5th)

- o Other restaurants offer prix fixe menus which you may notice as you walk past. Many provide a 3-course meal at reasonable, if not inexpensive, prices. A Cheapo's got to live a little, right?

For Snobs

Parisian restaurants might be close to heaven for those of the Snob variety. According to estimates, over one hundred restaurants in the City of Light have been granted one to three stars by the famous Michelin guide. However, that number can vary from year to year. While I mainly agree with the late journalist A. J. Liebling that this rating system has relegated "art to business," there are special occasions when nearly everyone feels like having an extremely elegant meal... if only to see how the élite actually live. So here are a few suggestions (out of a staggering number of comparable places) for possible extravagances to enjoy in person or just to experience vicariously by reading about them.

- Follow in the footsteps of famous Americans of the past: Montparnasse was THE place to be for members of the Lost Generation following World War I. Dining at one or more of the grand cafés in this area will certainly provide you with bragging rights as well as a decent meal.

  - o Le Dome, La Rotonde, La Coupole, and Le Select are clustered together along the boulevard du Montparnasse which straddles the 6th and the 14th arrondissements just off the boulevard Raspail

  - o Another favorite of expatriate Americans of the past, Closerie des Lilas, is located at 171, boulevard du Montparnasse (6th), a ten-minute walk east of the others. If you go to this location, check out the brass plaque at the bar with E. Hemingway inscribed on it.

In and around the Second World War Saint-Germain became popular with the French as well as foreign expats—think Camus, Sartre, and Beauvoir as well as Baldwin, Wright, and Picasso. As was the case in Montparnasse, these famous cafés on the boulevard Saint-Germain near the intersection with the rue de Rennes are located quite near each other in the 6th.

- ○ Café de Flore, 172, boulevard Saint-Germain
- ○ Les Deux Magots, 6, place Saint-Germain-des-Prés
- ○ Brasserie Lipp, 151, boulevard Saint-Germain

- • Go to the Gare de Lyon: It may seem strange to think of fine dining in a train station, but the Train Bleu (12th) has been going strong since the Exposition Universelle of 1900. Keep in mind that, like many of the previously described bouillons, the outstanding décor (in this case the pre-WWI Belle Époque) usually receives more enthusiastic reviews than its cuisine.

- • Reserve a table at a restaurant in a luxury hotel: For a combination of excellent food in beautiful surroundings—as long as you're prepared for sticker shock—choose a meal at one or more of the following. Again, be forewarned: the bill per person will add up to hundreds of euros before beverages.

  - ○ Le Cinq or Le George at the Four Seasons George V (8th)
  - ○ Épicure at Hôtel Bristol (8th)
  - ○ Apicius at Hotel Schneider (8th)
  - ○ Le Meurice Alain Ducasse (1st)
  - ○ Alain Ducasse au Plaza Athénée (8th)
  - ○ Les Univers de L'Espadon at the Ritz (1st)—where you can look for the Bar Hemingway as well.

- • Rub elbows with celebrities: Yes, the stars are out all over Paris. Once again, it goes without saying, money should be no object when choosing to dine at any of their favorite hangouts.

  - ○ Overlooking the Seine and Notre-Dame, the historic Tour

d'Argent (5th) once attracted the likes of Franklin Roosevelt, Marlene Dietrich, and Charlie Chaplin

○ The romantic Jules Verne (7th), on the second level of the Eiffel Tower, has been visited by Rihanna, Hugh Jackman, and Jennifer Aniston, among many others

○ L'Avenue (8th) has hosted Catherine Deneuve, Beyoncé, and Denzel Washington

○ Fouquet's (8th) was the choice for celebs like Bruce Willis and Liza Minnelli

○ Maxim's (also in the 8th) past clients include Barbra Streisand, John Travolta, and Lady Gaga

- Check out one of the most expensive restaurants (and supposedly the best) in the world: If you have the means and the interest, the Michelin-starred Guy Savoy (6th), has six sumptuous dining rooms, offering views of the Louvre, the Pont Neuf, and l'Institut de France, home to the Académie Française. Be sure to bring your appetite along if you want to try the thirteen-course menu at a whopping price of $550…as of this date. A more "reasonable" idea is to go there for lunch—still around $150 for three courses with a glass of wine being quite the bargain at about ten dollars a glass.

In closing I'd like to say that the French expression *rapport qualité prix* refers to the price/quality ratio. That is, does the meal seem to be a good value for the money? I'll leave it for you to decide where you'd find your comfort level in any of the above suggestions.

Chapter 3

Interesting Attractions

NATURALLY, PARIS HAS MUCH more to offer visitors than simply the well-documented sites such as the Louvre, the Eiffel Tower, and the Arc de Triomphe. To give you an idea, according to estimates, around 130 museums, nearly 200 churches, and over 400 parks and gardens dot the landscape of the capital. Now that would keep any tourist busy for quite some time! This chapter features remarkable locations within and outside of the city limits. There's the gorgeous Opéra Garnier, the Panthéon mausoleum which honors great citizens of the past (many who are discussed in later sections of this book), and les Invalides, a military complex containing several museums as well as the burial place of Napoléon Bonaparte. Five other museums explored here run the gamut from the fine arts to fashion, science, and household furnishings. In addition, we take a look at the homes of celebrated nineteenth-century authors Honoré de Balzac and Victor Hugo, the Saint-Sulpice church, and, for those prepared to travel an hour's drive south of the city, the striking Château de Fontainebleau. So have some fun discovering these twelve attractions.

L'Opéra Garnier

Admirers of Andrew Lloyd Webber's *Phantom of the Opera* might enjoy taking a tour of its setting, the so-called Palais Garnier. Even those unfamiliar with the musical will find the palace-like opulence of this opera house well worth a trip. The impetus to construct the building came as the result of an assassination attempt on the life of Napoléon III in 1858. Understandably wanting to build a space safer than the previous location of the opera, the emperor soon announced a competition to find a suitable architect. Out of 170 plans submitted, those by young Charles Garnier were unanimously accepted in 1861. The chosen site resolved an awkward convergence of streets but caused headaches for the architect because the high water table necessitated a double foundation. The façade, purposely hidden from view until the 1867 Exposition Universelle, revealed deities of Greek mythology, bronze busts between the columns of great composers like Mozart, Bach, and Beethoven, and Apollo holding his lyre between Harmony and Poetry at the very top. When an annoyed Empress Eugénie scornfully asked what kind of style it was supposed to be, the quick-thinking Garnier called it "Napoléon III." Construction, which had come to a halt during the Franco-Prussian War, was finally completed in January 1875. It was then that the curious public first caught sight of the interior. Its eclectic architecture left "no space without decoration:" the baroque sumptuousness of the white marble Grand Staircase with its red and green marble balustrade and two female torch holders, the omnipresent gold leaf, red velvet box seating, cherubs and nymphs, and its Grand Foyer with paintings devoted to music. The horseshoe-shaped auditorium still contains the large chandelier designed by Garnier. The ceiling of the space, however, was redone in 1964 by Marc Chagall and installed on a removable frame over the original. Classified a historical monument in 1923, the most expensive building of the Second Empire is considered a masterpiece by nearly everyone who sees it—however, predictably, it was extremely disliked by functionalist Swiss architect Le Corbusier. Many buildings have been modeled after the Opéra Garnier throughout the world, including the Thomas Jefferson Building of the Library of Congress in Washington D.C. Since the opening of the Opéra Bastille in 1989, the Garnier has been primarily used for ballet performances...which may remind spectators of Degas's famed portraits of ballerinas in its rehearsal rooms. Self-guided tours cost fourteen euros and a visit with a guide is just three euros more. The opera house is free (and quite crowded) on the first Sunday of the month. A restaurant and the Opera Library Museum are open to the public.

Address: place de l'Opéra, métro Opéra

Le Panthéon

The history of the Panthéon reflects France's political turmoil of the past. Originally designed as a church dedicated to Paris's patron saint Geneviève, with the advent of the French Revolution plans changed. By the 1790s the Latin Quarter landmark had become a mausoleum celebrating distinguished citizens such as Voltaire and Rousseau. Over the next century the Panthéon switched back and forth more times than one can count according to the regime in power: between church and mausoleum; with a cross or a flag on the top; the motto "A grateful nation honors its great men" coming and going. The Panthéon finally settled down for good as a mausoleum in 1881—becoming the final resting place of author Victor Hugo four years later. Way back, it was a mountain-top Roman forum which gave way to King Clovis's sixth century monastery dedicated to Saint Geneviève. By 1758 King Louis XV decided to replace the dilapidated structure and called upon Jacques-Germain Soufflot to design it. The architect, having studied in Italy, wanted the Neoclassical church to rival St. Peter's in Rome and St. Paul's in London. One of the most important architectural achievements of its day, it was built in the form of a Greek cross, with a triple dome made entirely of stone, a massive triangular religious pediment supported by twenty-four Corinthian columns, with flying buttresses and windows to bring in a maximum of light. Due to financial difficulties, the church took nearly thirty years to build and Soufflot didn't live to see its completion. He might be quite surprised to find that his pediment has been replaced with secular figures (statesmen, scholars, and military) and that lower windows have been bricked up and upper ones frosted to give the interior a more appropriately dark, funereal look. Astronomer Léon Foucault tested his pendulum to illustrate the rotation of the earth under the Panthéon's central dome in 1851. When the Catholic Church complained, the pendulum was removed but ultimately a copy was returned. As of this date, seventy-eight individuals (five of them women) are interred here. Some of the most famous, besides the aforementioned, are Émile Zola, Louis Braille, and the Curies. In 2002 Président Jacques Chirac corrected an injustice by having the remains of mixed-race author Alexandre Dumas transferred to the mausoleum. Except for a few holidays, the Panthéon is open daily from 10:00 a.m. to 6:00 p.m. (or 6:30 p.m. in summer); audio tours are available. Because of the site's popularity, reserve e-tickets in advance and arrive early morning mid-week, if possible. Visitors shouldn't miss the beautiful view from the colonnade. Tickets are priced at about twelve euros with a trip to the rooftop for an additional, minimal fee.

Address: place du Panthéon (5th), métro Cardinal-Lemoine or Saint-Michel; RER Luxembourg

L'Église Saint-Sulpice

Fans of *The Da Vinci Code* will probably want to put Saint-Sulpice high on their must-see list in Paris. The best-selling book and its film have made this a very popular tourist attraction—however, a note on display in the church points out the many inaccuracies in Dan Brown's novel. For one, the "pagan temple" originally said to have existed on this spot was actually a humble twelfth-century Catholic church named for a French saint. Rebuilt in the seventeenth and eighteenth centuries, the new church's façade was designed to resemble St. Paul's in London. When the exterior's designer died before completing the project, changes were initiated by subsequent architects...and then the French Revolution broke out. The result being that the two towers don't match and the right one remains unfinished—which many feel disrupts the edifice's overall harmony. The large pediment which once stretched between the towers was destroyed by lightning and never replaced. Out in the square it's hard to overlook the large fountain dedicated to four religious figures of the seventeenth century, the most famous being Bossuet and Fénelon. Inside the church, there's a lot to see. Two halves of an enormous shell function as holy water fonts near the entrance. To the right, there's a side chapel with murals by renowned artist Delacroix who also painted St. Michael slaying the dragon on the overhead vault. The lovely, ornate pulpit and the large pipe organ are worth checking out. In fact, music lovers might want to make it a point to come by at noon any Sunday for a free organ concert. At the front of the church visitors definitely don't want to miss the gnomon, an astronomical measurement device installed in 1727 to help determine the full moon and thus the date of Easter. Which brings us to another thing: in his literary account Brown took liberties with the brass line on the floor which was never called "the Rose Line" and has nothing to do with the Paris Meridian. Be that as it may, it's interesting to see the window which allows the sun's ray inside, the white marble obelisk, and the brass line of the gnomon whose technology has become obsolete with the advent of modern telescopes. The second biggest church in Paris after Notre-Dame, Saint-Sulpice has been the scene of several important historical events: from Victor Hugo's marriage to funeral masses for President Jacques Chirac and actress Mireille Darc. Free tours in French take place every Sunday at 2:30 p.m. A visit in English is available on the first Sunday of the month after the organ concert at around 12:45 p.m.; reserve this tour in advance by sending an email to visites@pssparis.net.

Address: 2, rue Palatine (6th), métro Saint-Sulpice

Les Invalides

On the Left Bank of the Seine facing the Pont Alexandre III stands an immense complex crowned by a gold dome. The construction of this masterpiece of classical French architecture was ordered by Louis XIV in 1670 to serve as a retirement home and hospital for elderly or injured military men. But before giving "The Sun King" too much credit for his humanitarian concern, it should be noted that there were political motives involved as well. Many soldiers who had served in the Thirty Years' War were upsetting the public by begging on the streets and getting into fights around the city. In order to improve his image with the populace as well as with his former troops, the king asked for plans to be submitted to build the Hôtel des Invalides on the once suburban plain of Grenelle. Out of the eight proposed designs, the one by the royal architect Libéral Bruant was selected. In a remarkably short period of three years the lodging, refectory, and infirmary were built; the planned royal chapel and its golden dome both designed by architect Jules Hardouin-Mansart, however, took an additional thirty years to finish. Besides a hospital and a retirement home, the structure housed a mausoleum, a print shop, and a plant for manufacturing uniforms. The extensive grounds of the esplanade attracted Parisians out for a stroll.

Several important historical events have taken place here. At the onset of the French Revolution in 1789, rioters seized twenty-seven canons and 32,000 muskets from the location, using them to storm the Bastille prison. In 1861, nearly forty years after Napoléon Bonaparte's death in exile on the island of Saint Helena, his remains were returned to Les Invalides; a twenty-year excavation project was needed to dig out a crypt under the dome for room to place his red tomb and its green granite base. In 1894 its Cour d'honneur was the scene of the degradation of Alfred Dreyfus, a wrong that was righted in the same spot twelve years later. (Read more about Captain Dreyfus in Chapter 12.) The building now houses a small hospital, a graveyard, military offices, and three museums including the popular Musée de l'Armée. The Saint-Louis-des-Invalides cathedral, originally built for the soldiers, maintains an old tradition of having war trophies lining the vault. The gold dome, a triumph of baroque architecture modeled on St. Peter's in Rome, was re-covered with gold in 1989 to commemorate the bicentennial of the French Revolution. Those interested in history and the military will be happy to pay the fourteen euros to visit Les Invalides; others may be content to sit on the grass of the esplanade and have a picnic.

Address: 129, rue de Grenelle (7th), métro Invalides, Varenne, or La Tour-Maubourg

Le Musée Marmottan Monet

In the 1990s the Marmottan added Monet to its title. While this museum does indeed have the world's largest collection of the artist's paintings, the name is a bit misleading. Because here you'll find one of the city's largest Impressionist and Post-Impressionist collections: art by Degas, Manet, Renoir, Gauguin, Caillebotte, and Boudin, to name but a few. The Marmottan also claims the prize for having the most works by the Grande Dame of Impressionism, Berthe Morisot. So how did all this come about? Originally in 1882, Jules Marmottan, a businessman and amateur art lover, purchased a small house on this spot near the Bois de Boulogne. When his son, lawyer turned art historian Paul Marmottan inherited the property, he bought up adjoining land in 1910 to create a mansion to display the family's collection of Napoleonic art and furniture. Not having any descendants, he arranged to give the building and its contents to the Académie des Beaux-Arts at the time of his death. By 1934 the Académie, having turned the house into a museum, began soliciting funds and donations. Six years later something quite remarkable happened. A female donor proposed to provide the museum with eleven Impressionist works, including the painting that gave the nineteenth-century movement its name: Monet's "Impression Sunrise." Accepting this gift marked a huge turning point on the part of the Académie. Since 1870 the Fine Arts institution had seen little value in Impressionist paintings, even going so far as to refuse those works at its annual salon. Then again in 1966 Monet's son Michel, also childless, bequeathed the works he owned from his father to the Marmottan. A new room, built under the garden of the mansion in 1970, displays the evolution of Monet's style up to and including some of the artist's famous waterlilies, created at the end of his life. In the early and mid-1990s the grandchildren of Berthe Morisot donated twenty-five of her paintings, seventy-five watercolors, and multiple pastels and drawings to the collection.

A frightening event for workers and visitors occurred here in 1985. In broad daylight five masked, armed men from a transnational organized crime syndicate burst into the museum and stole nine paintings—"Impression Sunrise" as well as others by Renoir and Morisot. It was a well-planned, targeted theft. Fortunately, no one was injured and five years later all of the works were discovered and restored to the exhibit. The museum, which is open Tuesday to Sunday 10:00 a.m. to 6:00 p.m., charges a hefty twenty-one euros per ticket.

Address: 2, rue Louis Boilly (16th), métro La Muette or Ranelagh, RER Boulainvilliers

La Maison Balzac

Lovers of Balzac would probably enjoy a visit to this small museum. After the author's home in suburban Sèvres was seized by creditors, he decided to move closer toward the city limits of Paris. He found a perfect spot on a hill near the Seine in what was then called the village of Passy. Not only was there a complicated entrance from its address on the rue Raynouard, but also a back exit onto the rue Berton providing for a hasty escape, if need be, from those pesky bill collectors. To conceal his identity, he decided to adopt the last name of his housekeeper/lover. So, it was "Monsieur Breugnol" who occupied a five-room apartment on the top floor of the building from 1840 to 1847. During that time, the acclaimed author wrote or edited many of the ninety works he incorporated into his masterpiece *La Comédie Humaine*. In 1908 another writer living at this location thought it would be wise to turn Balzac's only remaining home in the French capital into a museum; five years later the building received historical monument status and was eventually taken over by the city. The nineteenth-century structure itself hasn't changed: the size and layout of the rooms, the stained-glass windows, a black marble fireplace, and the parquet floor are still in place. Although most of Balzac's furniture has long since disappeared, the museum contains a couple of interesting pieces. The author's small work table, for example, complete with annotated page proofs in his handwriting is on display. And there's his armchair which, he once pointed out, "saw all of my misery, wiped away all of my tears." Visitors will also see the coffee pot marked with the initials HB, which undoubtedly provided his essential fifty or so cups per day. In the bedroom we find Balzac's gold and turquoise knobbed walking cane. Additionally, there are artifacts such as a 1842 daguerreotype of Balzac, artworks he purchased during his lifetime, and busts of the author by different sculptors including one by Rodin. The library on the ground floor has a wonderful collection of manuscripts, illustrations, and first editions of Balzac's works, as well as books that he annotated and signed, and even nineteenth-century newspapers. The charming garden with its view of the Eiffel Tower is popular with tourists as well as neighbors seeking a quiet place to relax. The Maison Balzac, which is open Tuesday to Sunday 10:00 a.m. to 6:00 p.m., is free of charge although there is a fee for temporary exhibits. Renovations in 2019 added a café and made the site handicap-accessible. (Read more about Balzac in Chapter 7.)

Address: 47, rue Raynouard (16th), métro Passy or La Muette; RER avenue du Président Kennedy

Le Château de Fontainebleau

For those neither interested in making the two-hour journey to see the châteaux of the Loire, nor in fighting the huge crowds at Versailles, here's a fitting and grand alternative. This current UNESCO World Heritage Site was once described by Napoléon Bonaparte as "the work of centuries, the home of kings." How right he was. For Fontainebleau was the only residence to be inhabited by an unbroken line of French monarchs for nearly 800 years. Most royals preferred the comforts of this castle even though they had plenty of other extravagant residences at their disposal. After serving as a humble, hunting lodge for kings since the twelfth century, Fontainebleau was updated by the king François 1er, freshly returned from the wars in Italy. In 1528 he began renovating the structure in the magnificent Renaissance style he had found there. One can still find his initial "F" and trademark salamander around the property. Since that time, other kings and emperors made additions…to the point that there are now over 1,500 rooms, (some of which are open to the public) on over 250 acres of land. And somehow the diverse styles manage to merge into a harmonious whole. Visitors will admire the richness and variety of the buildings and the décor of the most well-appointed castle in Europe. Much of the furniture is original, thanks to Napoléon who had missing objects tracked down and brought back to Fontainebleau. Apartments, ball rooms, great halls, and chapels are included in the entrance fee. Just looking around at the details—frescos, frames, walls, even ceilings and doors—is a delight. The château houses four museums, including an especially nice one devoted to Empress Eugénie's collection of Chinese artifacts. Guided tours (some in English) are often conducted for viewing special areas such as Marie Antoinette's Turkish boudoir (also used by Bonaparte's Joséphine) and Napoléon III's theater; in summer it's a good idea to reserve a tour in advance. After exploring the palace, don't miss a stroll around Louis XIV's large formal gardens. English audio tours are available for rent and provide a great introduction to the palace's history. Fontainebleau is open every day from 9:30 a.m. to 5:00 p.m. (or 6:00 p.m. depending on the time of year)—except on Tuesdays when it is closed as well as on a few holidays. Snobs might spring for 450 euros to treat a few friends to being picked up by a van at their hotel in Paris for a four – and-a-half-hour tour of the palace. Cheapos would undoubtedly prefer taking the forty-minute train ride from the Gare de Lyon then a bus to the castle for about twenty-five euros roundtrip, then purchasing a twelve-euro admission ticket at the door.

Address: place Charles de Gaulle, Fontainebleau—about an hour's drive southeast of Paris.

La Maison Victor Hugo

As far as free museums go in Paris, this is one of the best. How could it miss really with its fine artifacts, furniture, manuscripts, drawings, and photos associated with one of France's most celebrated authors? All of this in a lovely setting right on the place des Vosges. In 1832 when Hugo was thirty years old, he moved into the second floor of this building with his wife and four children. In nearly sixteen years at this address the great novelist, poet, and statesman did a lot of writing—poetry, plays, and a large portion of his very successful novel *Les Misérables*. Although there have been renovations to the apartment in the years since Hugo's days here, museum curators have done a good job arranging much of its collection based on archives and drawings. The visit, which covers various stages of the author's life, evolves in chronological order following a timeline of before, during, and after his years in exile. The antechamber focuses on Hugo's youth: his marriage and children, up to the time of the creation of his first literary work. The Red Lounge, a second "before exile" location, is a reconstruction of a meeting place where the author used to discuss literature, art, and politics with friends. Both the living room and dining room evoke his time as an expatriate in the Channel Island of Guernsey off the coast of Normandy. The first space shows the "interior decorator" side of Hugo. He designed a Chinese-style home for his longtime mistress Juliette Drouet who followed him and his family into exile; along with a table he gave her, one can see the lovers' initials VH and JD throughout the décor. The dining room with its Gothic-inspired furniture gives visitors the feeling of stepping back into the past. Some of the items on display throughout the apartment include a bust of the author by Rodin, Hugo's standup desk which he had built to do his writing, and a Sèvres vase presented to him as a gift from the government on the occasion of his eightieth birthday. Grandchildren of the author donated furniture from his last residence on the avenue d'Eylau (a street now renamed for the author) to recreate the bedroom where the author died. Important renovations took place at the museum in 2019 which added, among other things, an elevator making the space more handicap-accessible. Permanent collections are free as are temporary exhibits for visitors over age sixty. Audio guides are available at a minimal cost. La Maison Victor Hugo is open from Tuesday through Sunday, 10:00 a.m. to 6:00 p.m.—the last admission being at 5:40 p.m. (Check out the author's biography in Chapter 7.)

Address: 6, place des Vosges, formerly place Royale (4th), métro Bastille, Saint-Paul, or Chemin Vert

Le Musée Jacquemart-André

Part of the fascination of this museum is the story of the two people who created it: Édouard André and Nélie Jacquemart. The son of an affluent Protestant banking family, André was a soldier, politician, and, most importantly, an art collector. In 1868 he paid 1.5 million francs for land on the newly-created boulevard Haussmann to build his dream home. In 1872 André asked a well-known portraitist Cornélie Jacquemart to paint his picture. Jacquemart had come from a family of modest means but, through the encouragement of a wealthy woman, pursued art lessons. By the time she was thirty, the artist proved her determination and talent: by studying in Italy, having paintings accepted at the academic Salon, and even receiving Salon medals on three separate occasions. Nine years after creating André's portrait she married him, abandoning her career in order to host receptions, concerts, and help her husband purchase additional works of art. Besides an interest in the Italian Renaissance, the couple traveled throughout Europe and even to Egypt and Turkey to find new pieces for the collection. After André's death in 1894, his wife only possessed a handwritten will which allowed her to stave off his family's claims to his fortune. Because they had no children, the couple bequeathed their mansion and its contents to the Institut de France which opened it as a public museum in 1913, one year after her death. Not surprisingly, the house itself is a work of art. Architect Henri Parent, in fact, hoped to create a building to rival the Opéra Garnier. Before entering the museum, take the time to admire the beautiful façade. Once inside you'll find French art and decorative arts from the seventeenth century in the State Rooms, which the couple used for extravagant, formal receptions. A space they reserved for their close friends is the Italian Museum, which contains the Sculpture Gallery, the Florentine Gallery chapel, and the Venetian Gallery. Not to be missed are the Winter Garden, which despite its name is an indoor parlor filled with exotic plants, and a double-spiral staircase lined with frescoes by Tiepolo. Many of the beautifully furnished Informal Apartments—like the tapestry room, the study, and the library—had unique functions, such as for business meetings and consulting catalogs to plan for future purchases. Overall, much of the collection is comprised of works by leading artists such as Rembrandt, Fragonard, Gainsborough, and Botticelli. The museum, which costs twelve euros, is open daily 10:00 a.m. to 6:00 p.m. except on Mondays during exhibition period when it's open until 8:30 p.m. Guided tours in French and English are available as well as a very nice café in the former dining room.

Address: 158, boulevard Haussmann (8th), métro Miromesnil or Saint-Philippe-du-Roule

Le Musée des Arts et Métiers

Created around the time of the French Revolution, this museum is a testament to that era's rejection of religion in favor of technology. During those turbulent years at the end of the eighteenth century, the monks at Saint-Martin-des-Champs were dispersed and the state appropriated its medieval buildings for use as a prison. While the dormitories and most of the walls were destroyed, a museum was established in 1794 in the remaining nave and refectory to serve as a "technical temple," preserving and displaying scientific instruments and inventions. One of the world's oldest cultural institutions of its type, Arts et Métiers has received a steady stream of donations over the centuries. So many, in fact, that in years past numerous objects had been randomly stored in attics, cellars, and closets in the area of the nearby rue Saint-Martin. Its collection of over 80,000 objects and 15,000 drawings necessitated the creation of a vast storage building in the northern suburb of Saint-Denis in the early 1990s as well as a substantial addition to the abbey which was completed in 2000. In the museum approximately 2,500 objects, including monumental pieces, which haven't been moved from their original site, are divided into seven sections. Such diverse and interesting items as astrolabes, versions of Blaise Pascal's seventeenth-century mechanical calculator, chemist Antoine Lavoisier's laboratory, and Auguste Bartholdi's earliest model of the Statue of Liberty are part of the collection. The museum itself is mentioned at the end of Umberto Eco's 1988 novel *Foucault's Pendulum* because that astronomer's original device to prove the rotation of the earth has been on display here since getting booted from the Panthéon in 1855. Unfortunately, the pendulum was irreparably damaged in 2010 when its cable unexpectedly snapped sending the hefty brass bob crashing through the museum floor. In the transportation section there's a mixture of old French locomotives, steamship engines, and automobiles. Early airplanes are suspended from the ceiling, including aviation pioneer Clément Ader's bi-motor Avion 3 which he managed to get airborne for a few meters in the fall of 1897. Pilot Louis Blériot presented his aircraft to the museum just a few weeks after his historic flight over the English Channel in 1909. (You'll find more on Blériot in Chapter 13.) Open Tuesday to Sunday 10:00 a.m. to 6:00 p.m. and till 9:30 p.m. on Thursdays, the museum charges a nine-euro fee which is waived on the first Sunday of the month and after 6:00 p.m. on Thursday. Arts et Métiers is also included as part of the Paris Museum Pass.

Address: 60, rue Réaumur (3rd), métro Arts et Métiers

Le Musée des Arts Décoratifs

Located in the northern Marsan wing of the Louvre, this museum is a bit of a misnomer. Besides its huge collection of beautiful and functional decorative arts, the institution shares its space with fashion and the fine arts. Founded in 1905, it has amassed so many hundreds of thousands of objects that it is only able to display about twenty percent of its holdings, others being stored in warehouses as well as in the basement of the museum. There is truly something for everyone at this bright, expansive museum. Its wide variety of items—some hailing from as early as the twelfth century—are assembled into a dozen different areas. Five chronological periods begin with the Middle Ages/Renaissance rooms made up of religious artifacts as well as an interesting end-of-the-fifteenth-century bedroom; the seventeenth and eighteenth centuries' collection encompasses period room décors and entirely reconstructed ornate salons; the nineteenth century contains furniture, silverware, porcelain, as well as fine art; an Art Nouveau/Art Deco section covers among other things several stunning rooms from the home of haute couture designer Jeanne Lanvin; and a Modern/Contemporary section covers the years 1937 to the present. In addition, seven thematic departments (which are not all continually on view) include a jewelry gallery with pieces from Chanel, Cartier, Calder and Braque; glass articles—some created by Tiffany and Lalique; a wallpaper collection; kid-friendly games and toys from the mid-nineteenth century and beyond; fashions and textiles from designers such as Dior and Saint-Laurent. And so much more. The renovated museum is part of the bigger association MAD, (standing for *mode/*"fashion," *art*, and *design*) which is made up of several organizations including another museum and a library. The Loulou bar and restaurant as well as a bookstore and gift shop can be found on the premises. The museum, which has a fourteen-euro entry fee, is open Tuesday to Sunday 11:00 a.m. to 6:00 p.m., till 9:00 p.m. on Thursdays during exhibitions. Paris Pass is accepted.

Address: 107, rue de Rivoli (1st), métro Palais Royal-Musée du Louvre, Tuileries, or Pyramides

Le Palais Galliera, Musée de la Mode

Given that Paris is world-renowned as a capital of fashion, it's not at all surprising that there's a museum dedicated to that industry. Yet, the Palais Galliera didn't start out that way. The extremely wealthy Genovese Duchess of Galliera, Maria Brignole-Sale de Ferrari, had been generously involved in philanthropy since her husband's death in 1876. She decided to have a museum built at her expense to house her vast and important collection of paintings and sculptures, furniture, and pieces from Sevrès and Gobelins—all of which she would bequeath to the French state. But the notary writing up the donation made a major error deeding the property to the City of Paris which was discovered after construction was well underway. In addition, the duchess, a descendent of the French House of Orléans, was outraged by a new law set to expel direct royal heirs from the country.

Unable to take back the gift of the museum, she paid for its completion but took her art with her to Genoa. The building, designed in the Renaissance-style of an Italian palace the duchess owned, was elegant but rather small for a museum, raising the question of what exactly to do with it. At first in 1895 the Palais Galliera opened as an industrial design museum. By the mid-1950s the refurbished structure allowed for displaying works by prominent artists of the time. For several years beginning in 1960 it served as an auction house, finally settling down to its current state as a fashion museum in 1977. The extreme fragility of fabric when exposed to light was a huge issue, requiring rotating exhibits instead of permanent displays; recent renovations, however, have created a Salle Gabrielle-Chanel in the basement to protect and display styles from that design house. Examples of fashions from the eighteenth century to today run the gamut from haute couture and prêt-à-porter to uniforms and work clothes. Accessories include jewelry, hats, canes, fans, purses, scarves, and gloves—including a pair once owned by actress Sarah Bernhardt. (Read about her in Chapter 4.) The special exhibits are often designed according to themes (such as marriage, jeans, Paris fashions of the 1930s), sometimes devoted to a single person (like Marlene Dietrich), or naturally dedicated to a designer (Jacques Fath or Hubert de Givenchy, for example—both found in Chapter 10 of this book). For information about the current showing, contact the website: www.palaisgalliera.fr. During exhibitions the Palais Galliera is open every day except Mondays and holidays and has a ten-euro entry fee; otherwise, the museum is closed.

Address: 10, avenue Pierre-1er-de-Serbie (16th), métro Iéna or Alma-Marceau

Introduction to Famous French Residents of Paris

F. Scott Fitzgerald once remarked about his fellow citizens, "The best of America drifts to Paris." The same can obviously be said about the finest from France. During the nineteenth and twentieth centuries, which is our focus, the capital saw an influx of many of the country's greatest professionals—be it in the arts, literature, cuisine, music or fashion, to name but a few. But the World War II era was an extremely stressful and difficult period for the French. There were heroes among them, of course. People like Charles Aznavour, Albert Camus, and Marcel Marceau risked their lives in order to protect their fellow citizens from the Nazis. Photographer Janine Niépce developed films of German defensive positions. *The Little Prince* author Antoine de Saint-Exupéry died while flying a reconnaissance mission for the French Air Force in 1944. On the other hand, many had their reputations blemished by their failure to speak up; Sartre and Beauvoir immediately come to mind. Others, because of their anti-Semitic or pro-Nazi views, actively collaborated with the occupying powers. The head of the Vichy government, Philippe Pétain, was no more than a puppet of the Germans. Recently discovered documents show that Coco Chanel acted as a Nazi agent. In the following pages then you will see a portrait of the times—the good with the bad. If any of your favorites are missing, it might be that they're too recent to have published biographies or that I wasn't able to find addresses for them while doing my research. Here's hoping you will recognize some familiar names and enjoy being introduced to unfamiliar ones.

Chapter 4

Actors and Directors

As IS OFTEN THE case with inventions and discoveries, people in a variety of countries were working simultaneously on creating the first motion picture camera. Americans Thomas Edison and Leland Stanford were among them along with France's Lumière brothers. Without a doubt, though, Georges Méliés was the first to envisage film as a narration. His hugely successful 1902 *Le Voyage dans la Lune* ("A Trip to the Moon") propelled France into the forefront of the emerging industry. Ever since the French have continued to play a significant role in the world of film with directors like Renoir, Godard, and Truffaut as well as actors such as Bardot, Deneuve, and Depardieu. In this chapter you'll learn about eleven important individuals in the history of French cinema, including Sarah Bernhardt who was mainly known as a theater actress but who also had a few film roles.

Brigitte Bardot (1934-)

B.B., as she is known, has been making headlines since the 1950s. From the pouty, "sex kitten" of film she evolved into a pop singer, an animal rights activist, and eventually a controversial anti-immigrant figure. Growing up in an affluent, strict Catholic family in the chic 16th arrondissement of Paris, she was encouraged to pursue music and dance lessons. Soon the girl turned to modeling, appearing on the cover of *Elle* magazine at age fifteen. Her photo caught the attention of filmmakers in the French capital who launched her movie career. Still a teenager, she fell in love with Roger Vadim, six years her senior. Her parents strongly objected to their daughter's marriage, but relented after Brigitte threatened suicide—as long as she waited to marry until she turned eighteen. Vadim directed his wife in *And God Created Woman* in 1956 which made her an international star. Men all over the world were enthralled by her beauty and flocked to see her mainly mediocre films. So attractive was she that in 1969 the French state for the first time used the image of an actual person to embody the national symbol *Marianne*. In the '60s Bardot began starring in musical shows and recorded several popular songs. By 1973, however, she decided that she'd had enough of the limelight: "My soul is not my own anymore. I cannot live like I want to. I am going to give up films." In 1986 she devoted herself to her passion, the protection of animals, by setting up her foundation.

Addresses for Bardot

- 1, rue de la Pompe (16th)—address of her well-to-do family's very large apartment

- Cours Hattemer, 43, rue Decamps (16th)—starting at age seven, she attended this private school which allowed free time for extracurriculars such as ballet classes

- La Tour Paris, 86, rue de La Tour (16th)— Bardot later went to this international Catholic high school

- Église Notre-Dame-de-Grâce de Passy, 10, rue de l'Annonciation (16th)—site of her 1952 wedding to Vadim

- 71, avenue Paul Doumer (16th)—Bardot lived in this building from 1956 to 1971 during which time she had an affair with actor Jean-Louis Trintignant and gave birth to her only child Nicolas, son of her second husband, actor Jacques Charrier

- Le Train Bleu, place Louis-Armand (12th)—she frequented this luxury restaurant in the Gare de Lyon

- 28, rue Vineuse (16th)—location of the *Fondation Brigitte Bardot* established for the protection of animals

Sarah Bernhardt (1844-1923)

The "Divine Sarah" didn't lack for epithets. Cocteau first used "un monstre sacré" to describe the theatrical giant, Hugo called her "the golden voice," and a biographer complained that she was "a notorious liar." Constant fabrications about her life and her violent temper were possibly due to her traumatic childhood. The illegitimate daughter of a fifteen-year-old courtesan (who was a largely absent mother), Sarah hardly knew her father. A doctor predicted that the sickly girl would die early, leading to an obsession with death from her teen years on: she even had a coffin displayed in her home throughout her life. When she threw a fit at the suggestion of marriage, her mother's lover declared that the girl was a born actress who should study at the Conservatory. That same night seeing a play at the Comédie Française she noted "the curtain of my life…was rising." In future roles like *Phèdre* and *Camille*, her raw emotion, perfect articulation, and exaggerated gestures had the public raving and in tears. With her traveling company formed in 1880, the actress began world tours including nine trips to the United States. Bernhardt, an excellent self-promoter, did ads for products from face powder to cigarettes. But she also showed great concern for the injured during the Franco-Prussian War and performed for troops at the Front in World War I, despite having had her gangrenous right leg amputated. Bernhardt was not granted a national funeral, yet the adoring crowds rivaled those of her friend Victor Hugo. The actress is one of the few French people with a star on Hollywood Walk of Fame.

Addresses for Bernhardt

- 5, rue de l'École de Médecine (6th)—a commemorative plaque marks the building where Henriette-Rosine Bernard was born (though both her birth name and birthplace have been disputed)
- 18, rue Boileau (16th)—she attended the former boarding school of Madame Fressard where she got her first start in theater

- Conservatoire de Paris d'art dramatique, 2 bis, rue du Conservatoire (9th)—in 1859 she began a two-year program at the acting conservatory

- Comédie Française, 1, place Colette (1st)—Bernhardt entered this theater as an actress in 1862 but was let go for slapping another performer; once she was successful, she was recalled here in 1874 only to quit again in 1880

- Odéon, place de l'Odéon (6th)—after leaving the Comédie Française, she spent six years at this theater, transforming the building into a hospital during the siege of Paris in 1870

- 16, rue Auber (9th) and 4, rue de Rome (8th)—as Bernhardt became more famous, she moved to larger apartments

- Théâtre de la Renaissance, 20, boulevard Saint-Martin (10th)—in 1893 she took over the management of this theater where she also performed

- Grand Hôtel, now the InterContinental Paris Le Grand, 2, rue Scribe (9th)—in December 1896 Sarah Bernhardt Day was partially celebrated with a meal for 500 guests at this hotel

- Théâtre Sarah-Bernhardt, now Théâtre de la Ville, 2, place du Châtelet (4th)—from 1899 she directed and performed at this theater whose name was later changed by the Nazis because of the actress's Jewish heritage

- 56, boulevard Pereire (17th)—she spent her last years at this address

- Cimetière du Père Lachaise, 16, rue du Repos (20th)—Bernhardt is buried in division 44 of this cemetery

Leslie Caron (1931-)

From her experience growing up in occupied Paris during World War II, Caron remembered there was "a shortage of everything: food, clothes, heat, water—hot or cold." Even as part of a well-to-do family, she suffered lingering effects from malnutrition. Who would have guessed that a mere decade later she would begin a career as one of the top artists of the '50s? Yes, indeed, Caron received many accolades for her talents as a dancer, singer, and actress—in both musical and dramatic roles. Despite the privations of her war-torn childhood, at age eleven she was able to begin taking ballet lessons. Five years later Caron became a member of a ballet company and one of her performances soon caught the attention of Gene Kelly. In a year the American actor/dancer was back in the capital to offer Caron the chance for a film contract with MGM. The teenager performed her first role opposite Kelly in the musical *An American in Paris*; the pair astounded audiences with a seventeen-minute ballet to the title song at the finale. During her seven years with the studio, Caron found it "very difficult to adapt" to Hollywood. Yet she had the good fortune to appear with some of the biggest names of the time, including Fred Astaire. Her final film with MGM, *Gigi*, starring Louis Jourdan and Maurice Chevalier, won her a Golden Globe nomination and a 1998 election to the Grammy Hall of Fame. Caron's book *Thank Heaven* recounts the times of her life.

Addresses for Caron

- 155, boulevard Saint-Germain (6th)—the family first lived at this address near the Brasserie Lipp

- 48, avenue Marceau (8th)—they then moved to the fifth floor in a handsome building at this location

- Institut de l'Assomption, 6, rue de Lübeck (16th)—she attended this Catholic school

- Théâtre des Champs-Élysées, 15, avenue Montaigne (8th)—at sixteen Caron had small solo parts after joining a ballet company run by Roland Petit

- Hôtel George V, 31, avenue George V (8th)—she first met with Gene Kelly at this five-star hotel to discuss *An American in Paris*

- Maxim's, 3, rue Royale (8th)—parts of *Gigi* were filmed at this restaurant as well as in place de la Concorde and the Bois de Boulogne

- Théâtre du Châtelet, place du Châtelet (1st)—in 2010 she played in *A Little Night Music* at this theater

Catherine Deneuve (1943-)

This well-known figure has a lot in common with Brigitte Bardot: both were actresses and models whose faces served as the national symbol of Marianne; both grew up in the chic 16th arrondissement of Paris; both have courted controversy with their outspoken political views (though primarily on opposite sides); both had a relationship with director Roger Vadim and both sued him when his tell-all autobiography told a little more than they liked. But Deneuve, born Catherine Dorléac in an acting family, apparently never tired of making films. After taking her mother's maiden name, the teenager began her long-lasting career. In over 100 films she received fourteen César nominations (the equivalent of the Oscars) and won the best actress César for *The Last Métro* (1980) and *Indochine* (1992). Considered the muse of Yves Saint-Laurent, the twenty-two-year-old Deneuve was first dressed by the designer for a visit with Queen Elizabeth; he later created her costumes for films like *Belle de Jour*. The actress has been the face of both Chanel No. 5 and L'Oréal Paris and has done ads for Louis Vuitton luggage. In 1963 and '65 Deneuve was the subject of *Playboy* magazine pictorials. She married only once—to British fashion photographer David Bailey. But Deneuve has had several relationships, including two which produced children: a son with Vadim and a look-alike daughter with Italian actor Marcello Mastroianni. The "Ice Maiden" published her private diaries in 2005 which disappointed some with its great gaps of time and lack of gossip.

Addresses for Deneuve

- 146, boulevard Murat (16th)—where she spent her childhood with her parents and three sisters

- Lycée La Fontaine, 1, place de la porte Molitor (16th)—Deneuve attended this secondary school

- rue Vineuse, number unknown (16th)—she lived here with her partner, director Roger Vadim

- 76, rue Bonaparte (6th) —in the '70s she moved to the sixth floor of this Left Bank address near the Saint-Sulpice church

- Marché Raspail, boulevard Raspail (6th)—she often visits this marché on Sundays

- Le Salon du Panthéon, 13, rue Victor-Cousin (5th)—Deneuve helped redesign this cinema

- Bon Marché, 24, rue de Sèvres (6th)—chic department store where she shops near her home

Gérard Depardieu (1948-)

Once describing himself as having a "hooligan side," this ubiquitous actor started out simply as a mischievous little boy called Pétarou (or "little firecracker") by members of his working-class family. The impish child quickly turned into a delinquent teenager selling stolen goods on the street and eventually an adult involved in several accidents and drunken brawls. In the meantime, however, he became serious about building his career as an actor. After quitting school at thirteen, Depardieu left his home in central France for Paris where he started acting at a small comedy theater in 1967. Film roles came pouring in as he developed into one of the most prolific actors in the history of French cinema. With more than 180 films under his belt, Depardieu has received seventeen César nominations, winning the best actor award for *The Last Metro* (1980) and *Cyrano de Bergerac* (1990), a movie for which he also received an Oscar nomination. Once established as an actor, he bought up luxurious properties, shops, and restaurants in Paris and vineyards in areas such as the Loire and Bordeaux. The heavy tax burden in France prompted his threat to give up his French passport along with an actual move across the border into Belgium in 2012. Soon afterwards, he befriended Vladimir Putin who granted the actor Russian citizenship. For his TV series *Bon Appétit*, which appeared in 2015 and 2016, the rotund epicure went around Europe investigating the history of food and regional specialties from disparate locales such as Brittany, Tuscany, Scotland, and the Basque Country.

Addresses for Depardieu

- Café de la Gare, 41, rue du Temple (4th)—Depardieu began his career at this dinner theater in the Marais where other French actors also got their start

- Hôtel de Chambon, 95, rue du Cherche-Midi (6th)—site of his former mansion, a historical monument dating from 1820, whose asking price was 50 million euros in 2012

- L'Écaille de la Fontaine, 15, rue Gaillon—one of Depardieu's restaurants near the Opéra Garnier, just opposite his former restaurant La Fontaine Gaillon, 1, rue de la Michodière (both in the 2nd); Depardieu's wine bar, the Bien Décidé, is located at 117, rue du Cherche-Midi (6th)

- Moby Dick, 50, rue du Cherche-Midi (6th)—he sold the one-time fish store he owned

Jean Gabin (1904-1976)

The subtitle of one biography calls Gabin *The Actor Who Was France*. With ninety-five films over a forty-five-year career, he was certainly one of the greats in French cinema. Born Jean-Gabin-Alexis Moncorgé in Paris, he spent most of his childhood in Mériel north of the city where a museum is now dedicated to him. Once he dropped out of high school, he took a series of low-paying jobs. His exasperated father, a cabaret entertainer, pulled some strings at the Folies-Bergère and got his son bit parts, or as Gabin put it, "playing lampposts in the distance." The nineteen-year-old Gabin's singing—which mimicked Maurice Chevalier—got him hired as actress/singer Mistinguett's partner at the Moulin Rouge. After performing in silent films and early talkies, true recognition came in the mid-1930s with the Canadian saga *Maria Chapdelaine*, the Algeria-based *Pépé le Moko*, and Jean Renoir's war classic *La Grande Illusion*. Early roles as a tragic, romantic working-class type revealed the actor's exceptional charisma. During the German Occupation, he retreated to Hollywood, but poor English skills greatly restricted his success in American movies. In

1941 he and actress Marlene Dietrich began a turbulent, eight-year romance. Serving in the French military from January 1944, Gabin was highly decorated but the experience changed him both morally and physically. With all-white hair he no longer felt capable of portraying romantic leads, taking parts as the gruff patriarch instead. In later years Gabin found success playing Georges Simenon's Inspector Maigret and Jean Valjean in Hugo's *Les Misérables*. Crowds and television crews attended his funeral after his death from leukemia.

Addresses for Gabin

- 23, boulevard de Rochechouart (9th)—he was born at this address
- Lycée Janson de Sailly, 106, rue de la Pompe (16th)—Gabin abandoned his studies at this high school
- Moulin Rouge, 82, boulevard de Clichy (18th)—cabaret where he performed with Mistinguett
- Hôtel Claridge, 74, avenue des Champs-Élysées (8th)—from a balcony in this hotel after Liberation he saw his former tank company parade down Paris's main street
- Salle Pleyel, 252, rue du Faubourg Saint-Honoré (8th)—in April 1954 to celebrate his fiftieth birthday and twenty-five years as an actor, a friend threw a party for Gabin and 2000 of his friends
- Cimetière du Père Lachaise, 16, rue du Repos (20th)—Gabin's body was cremated at this cemetery and then, with full military honors, his ashes were scattered at sea off the coast of Brest

Jean-Luc Godard (1930-)

This director turned the world of cinema upside down as part of the French New Wave movement. Godard was born in Paris before moving at age four with his wealthy family to Switzerland. From a young boy simply interested in sports, he became the black sheep of the family as an adolescent, stealing books or money which turned into a mania over time. Once he passed his high school exams, Godard enrolled as an archeology student at the Sorbonne. Instead of going to classes, however, he found his real passion in reading articles on film and attending ciné-clubs. There he "discovered a world which nobody had spoken to me about." And he wasn't alone. Surrounded by like-minded friends such as future directors Éric Rohmer and Jacques Rivette, he recalls that "in the 1950s cinema was as important as bread." At nineteen he founded the short-lived journal *Gazette du cinéma* and wrote articles in similar publications like André Bazin's *Cahier du* cinéma. After a series of short subjects, in 1960 he made the highly successful feature-length movie *Breathless* starring Jean-Paul Belmondo and Jean Seberg. Over the next seven years he continued turning out fresh, invigorating films by breaking some of the rules of the past. For example, he achieved a documentary feel by encouraging character asides, using jump-cuts, inventing dialog day to day, and mixing high and low culture—such as Shakespeare and Humphry Bogart. His political style of the late '60s and early '70s became more traditional a decade later. According to his first wife actress Anna Karina, Godard now lives as a recluse at his home on Lake Geneva.

Addresses for Godard

- 2, rue Cognacq-Jay (7th)—he was born at this address

- Lycée Buffon, 16, boulevard Pasteur (15th)—Godard studied here but failed the *bac* in 1947

- 78, rue d'Assas (6th)—while in high school he rented an apartment in the same building as writer Jean Schlumberger, a friend of the family

- Cinématique française, once found at 7, avenue de Messine (8th)—Godard met Truffaut and Rivette attending the film showings of Henri Langlois; he went to André Bazin's ciné-club at 5, rue des Ursulines (5th) as well as Rohmer's in the Salle des Société Savantes, 8, rue Danton (6th)

Georges Méliès (1861-1938)

Long before Lucas and Spielberg, there was Méliès. Although his name might not ring a bell for many today, this pioneer in the film industry employed a variety of special effects to create innovative, enormously successful fantasies like *A Trip to the Moon* (1902) and *The Impossible Voyage* (1904). As a student, he was often scolded by his teachers for sketching portraits and caricatures over his books instead of doing his school work. By age ten, he set about constructing puppet theaters and as a teenager began building marionettes. Méliès worked for a while at the family shoe factory after his father refused to finance his study of painting at the École des Beaux-Arts. A stay in London introduced him to magic which would become a lifelong love and a huge influence on his films. To draw bigger crowds to magic shows he put on throughout Paris, Méliès added melodrama and comedy, such as a professor who continues to talk even after he is decapitated. (A commentary on his past teachers, perhaps?) Inspired by the cinématographe camera of the Lumière brothers, Méliès acquired a projector in London which he was able to convert into a camera. He then began showing his short films at his Théâtre Robert-Houdin in the spring of 1896. Following his precept that "steady work overcame all things," he worked tirelessly between his theater and his Star Film Company for over seventeen years where he produced more than 500 short documentaries, comedies, dramas, satires, and some particularly popular fairy tales. Unfortunately, much of his work has been lost.

Addresses for Méliès

- 29, boulevard Saint-Martin (3rd)—a white plaque here notes the birthplace of Méliès

- Lycée Louis-le-Grand, 123, rue Saint-Jacques (5th)—he attended this prestigious secondary school

- Théâtre Robert-Houdin, formerly located at 8, boulevard des Italiens (9th)—Méliès presented his *soirées fantastiques* (magic shows) at this theater which he bought in 1888

- Musée Grévin, 10, boulevard Montmartre (9th) and the Galerie Vivienne, 5, rue de la Banque (2nd)—he performed magic shows at these two venues

- Cimetière du Père Lachaise, 16, rue du Repos (20th)—Méliès's recently renovated grave can be found in division 64 of this cemetery

Jean Renoir (1894-1979)

Like his famous father, Jean Renoir was an artist, one might say, who did his painting with a camera. At his death, both Orson Welles and Charlie Chaplin heaped words of admiration on their fellow filmmaker, describing him as the greatest director of all time. Now that's no small praise. But viewing Renoir's films such as *Grand Illusion* (1937), *The Rules of the Game* (1939), and *A Day in the Country* (1946), makes their evaluation understandable. The second of three sons, young Jean frequently appeared in his father's Impressionist paintings. The family moved south in 1907 and six years later Renoir received a degree in philosophy from the Université d'Aix-en-Provence. As an infantryman during World War I, he suffered an injury that would leave him with a permanent limp. While recovering, he spent a lot of time watching movies—which certainly had an impact on his future career. After dabbling in ceramics, Renoir married Andrée Heuschling (professionally known as Catherine Hessling) and decided to try his hand at filmmaking in order to make his wife a star. Starting out with silent movies, he turned to "talkies" in the early 1930s. His highly successful World War I classic, *La Grande Illusion*, became the first foreign film nominated in the best picture category at the Oscars. After the German invasion of France in 1940, Renoir fled to the U.S. where he continued his career, although he was often frustrated by the film studio he referred to as "Sixteenth Century Fox."

Addresses for Renoir

- 13, rue Girardon (18th)—birthplace of Renoir in the Château des Brouillards

- 33, rue de la Rochefoucauld (9th)—the family moved here two years after Jean's birth then lived at 43, rue Caulaincourt (18th) for a few years beginning in 1901

- 30, rue de Miromesnil (8th)—Renoir shared an apartment with the son of Paul Cézanne at this address

- Studio Gaumont, 10, rue Carducci (19th)—part of Renoir's movie *Nana* was filmed here

- Moulin Rouge, 82, boulevard de Clichy (18th)—the cabaret where the first showing of *Nana* took place

- Société des films Jean Renoir, 15, avenue Matignon (8th)—once the location of his film headquarters

- 4, avenue Frochot (9th)—Renoir's residence near the place Pigalle in Montmartre which he maintained from 1937 to 1969

Éric Rohmer (1920-2010)

Gilbert Cordier, Anthony Barrier, Sébastien Erms, and even Éric Rohmer are just a few of the pseudonyms used by one man: Maurice Schérer. Most biographers agree that the masking of his identity—which at times went as far as changing his birthdate and birthplace—was the director's way of preventing his judgmental family from discovering his real profession. Apparently, he grew up in Tulle, south of Limoges, where he showed intellectual curiosity in literature, art, and music. In the mid-1940s after moving to Paris, he worked as a teacher, wrote a novel, and freelanced as a journalist. The switch to film criticism came thanks to new friends who introduced him to the works of directors Renoir, Carné, and Hitchcock via ciné-clubs. In 1950 when someone asked why he didn't make his own movies, he borrowed a 16-millimeter camera and started turning out short subjects. Seven years later he and Claude Chabrol wrote *Hitchcock*, helping to establish the "auteur theory" which views the director as the major creative force in filmmaking. Over his long career Rohmer produced over twenty feature-length films, preferring to cluster them into cycles. His "Six Moral Tales" from the '60s and '70s, for instance, contain the internationally popular films *My Night at Maud's*, *Claire's Knee*, and *Love in the Afternoon*. As the "auteur" of these scripts, Rohmer created male characters "who like to analyze their thoughts and moods" while sorting out their complicated love life. "Le Grand Momo" (as his younger friends called Maurice) went on to establish two production companies: Les Films de Losange and Compagnie Éric Rohmer.

Addresses for Rohmer

- Lycée Henri IV, 23, rue Clovis (5th)—he was an average student but began reading great literature at this high school

- Hôtel de Lutèce, 4, rue Victor-Cousin (5th)—in 1943 he took a furnished room in this hotel keeping it for nearly fifteen years

- College Sainte-Barbe, once found at 4, rue Valette (5th)—he started out as a substitute classics teacher and remained for five years

- Café de Flore, 172, boulevard Saint-Germain-des-Prés (6th)—at this café he met Alexandre Astruc who wrote on cinema

- La Tribune de l'écran, formerly at 31, avenue de Pierre-1er-de-la-Serbie (16th)—Rohmer attended Thursday evening films here and at Objectif 49 film club's Sunday showings at the Broadway, 36, avenue des Champs-Élysées (8th)

- Cinématique française, once found at 7, avenue de Messine (8th)—he often visited this site where Henri Langlois taught cinéma and showed films

- 8, rue Danton (6th)—from '47 to '51 Rohmer organized the Ciné-Club du Quartier Latin in the Salle des Société Savantes where he met Godard and Rivette; he ran another club at the Cluny-Palace theater at 71, boulevard Saint-Germain (5th)

- Institut d'art et d'archéologie, 3, rue Michelet (6th)—from 1977 to 2001 he taught a film course at this institute

- Cimetière du Montparnasse, 3, boulevard Edgar Quinet (14th)—his grave in the 13th division of this cemetery is marked with his birth name as well as his most famous pseudonym

François Truffaut (1932-1984)

The 1959 film *The 400 Blows* focuses on a fictitious character

Antoine Doinel—an unloved child, who is disruptive in class, skips school, lies, steals, and ends up in a reformatory. Viewers may not realize that the movie reflects the real-life experiences of its director. Born in Montmartre to an unwed, teenaged mother, Truffaut was placed with a wet nurse until his grandmother noticed that the three-year-old was wasting away and brought him to live at her house. During the next seven years she instilled in her grandson an abiding love for books and music. After her death, his straightlaced grandfather insisted that the boy's mother and stepfather, Roland Truffaut, take him in. Their lack of attention toward the child eventually drove the rebellious adolescent into a life of petty crime. Quite a sad tale. But Truffaut had the intelligence, drive, and passion for cinema to be able to turn his story into art on the big screen. Like two of his cinematic heroes Alfred Hitchcock and Jean Renoir, he was a proponent of the "auteur theory," writing the scenario as well as directing the film. As one of the first (and possibly best) directors of the New Wave movement, he used portable equipment to create his documentary-type style. Truffaut received several French Césars for writing and directing. In 1974 his *Day for Night* won the Academy Award for "best foreign film." His life was cut short by a brain tumor at age fifty-two.

Addresses for Truffaut

- 21, rue Henry-Monnier (9ᵗʰ)—from 1935 until his grandmother died seven years later he lived with his grandparents at this address

- 33, rue de Navarin (9ᵗʰ)—for five years beginning in 1944 Truffaut lived here with his parents; note the memorial plaque on the building

- Albert Simpère et Compagnie, 16, avenue de l'Opéra (1ˢᵗ)—he took his first job in October 1946 as a "pen pusher and messenger," going between warehouses for this grain merchant; his parents took two-thirds of his pay

- Studio des Champs-Élysées, 15, avenue Montaigne (8ᵗʰ)—where he first saw Hitchcock's movie *Rope*

- Cluny-Palace, 71, boulevard Saint-Germain (5th)—location of the first film club Truffaut ran, Le Cercle Cinémane

- 82, rue Marcadet (18th)—the interior of an apartment at this address was used in the movie *Les 400 Coups*

- Théâtre Montmartre, now the Théâtre de l'Atelier, 1, place Charles Dullin (18th)—main setting for the film *Le Dernier Métro*

- Cimetière de Montmartre, 20, avenue Rachel (18th)—Truffaut is buried in division 21 of this cemetery

Chapter 5

Architects, Engineers, and City Planners

Just about anyone who goes to Paris comes away in awe of its striking architecture. It's hard not to be delighted by stunning relics of the past such as Notre-Dame, Sainte-Chapelle, and the Louvre. But there's a lot to celebrate from more recent history as well: The Eiffel Tower, of course, "the Iron Lady," a great, soaring symbol of the capital; the Opéra Garnier, so magnificent inside and out; several smaller copies of the Statue of Liberty, reminding us of the monumental gift from France to the U.S.; and even some elegant Art Nouveau métro entrances. Simply walking down the broad avenues, we notice the refinement and uniformity of the Haussmannian buildings which definitely contribute to the city's beauty. In the following pages, you will read about six important men who lived in Paris and contributed in some way to making the city what it is today.

Frédéric Auguste Bartholdi (1834-1904)

This guy did it all: drawing, painting, watercolor, photography, sculpture, and architecture. But Bartholdi is most famous for creating the colossus that was originally called "Liberty Enlightening the World." Today she is known solely as the Statue of Liberty. The Colmar native moved with his mother and brother to Paris after his father's untimely death. The nineteen-year-old Bartholdi, who studied with renowned artists and sculptors of the time, had a sculptural group accepted at the Paris Salon in 1853. A couple of years later he took off on a life-changing trip to Yemen and Egypt where he became interested in creating massive sculptures. His huge Lion de Belfort, for example, representing French resistance during the Franco-Prussian War, is located in the eastern town of the same name—with smaller copies in Montreal and in the 14th arrondissement of Paris. A visit to the U.S. in 1871 inspired Bartholdi to create a monument honoring the centennial of American independence. He incorporated symbols like the torch of enlightenment, the tablet of law, as well as broken chains under the statue's feet—all representing democracy and freedom. Between 1884 and '85 the Statue of Liberty could be seen gradually rising from the foundry rooftops in the 17th arrondissement where it was being built. The 225-ton sculpture, whose iron framework was designed by Gustave Eiffel, was then transported in pieces by ship to New York. The finished product was dedicated on October 28, 1886 with Bartholdi, who had supervised its assembly, and President Grover Cleveland in attendance. The sculptor remarked: "This thing will live for eternity."

Addresses for Bartholdi

- Lycée Louis-le-Grand, 123, rue Saint-Jacques (5th)—Bartholdi attended this prominent secondary school in Paris

- 16, rue Chaptal (9th)—he took painting classes at the studio of Dutch artist Ary Scheffer, now the address of the Musée de la Vie Romantique

- École des Beaux-Arts, 14, rue Bonaparte (6th)—Bartholdi studied architecture at this well-known fine arts school

- Lion de Belfort, place Denfert-Rochereau (14th)—this smaller, bronze version of the original is situated in the middle of the square dedicated to the colonel who commanded the troops during the Prussian attack on the town of Belfort near Mulhouse

- 25, rue de Chazelles (17th)—location of the former factory of

Gaget, Gauthier & Co. where Bartholdi assembled the Statue of Liberty; a commemorative plaque is located on the side of the building near the driveway. The architect's personal workshop was on the same street at #21

- 82, rue d'Assas (6th)—site of Bartholdi's last residence and studio near the Luxembourg Gardens

- 60, rue Réaumur (3rd)—his plaster model of the Statue of Liberty is located in the Arts et Métiers museum at this address; three small bronze replicas of the statue can be found around the city: on the Île aux Cygnes, an island in the Seine off the Pont de Grenelle (15th), on the west side of the Luxembourg Gardens (6th), and in the entrance hall to the Musée d'Orsay 5, quai Anatole France (7th)

Gustave Eiffel (1832-1923)

This renowned French engineer was actually descended from German roots. In fact, his birth certificate states his name as Alexandre Gustave Bonickhausen dit Eiffel. Hard to imagine, but if he hadn't officially changed to Eiffel in 1880, just seven years before working on his most famous structure, we might be speaking about the Bonickhausen Tower today. Doesn't exactly roll off the tongue, does it? Growing up in Dijon, three and a half hours south of the capital, young Gustave was surrounded by family and friends who encouraged his intellectual development. At twenty, he was accepted at two prestigious Grandes Écoles in Paris, finally deciding on the very selective École Centrale. The lengthy résumé of the so-called "magician of iron" includes everything from bridges and railway stations to churches and synagogues—in North and South America as well as all over Europe. Eiffel openly acknowledged that inspiration for his famed Parisian tower, the centerpiece at the 1889 Universal Exposition, came from the more prosaic (now defunct) Latting Observatory in New York City. Of his celebrated creation he would one day remark: "I ought to be jealous of the tower. She is more famous than I am." And that is undoubtedly true. Perhaps second only to the Eiffel Tower in popularity is his design of the metal framework of Bartholdi's Statue of Liberty, difficult to create because of the asymmetry of the statue's shape—one arm raised and the other bent. Bartholdi undoubtedly knew that Eiffel was the man to get the job done.

Addresses for Eiffel

- École Centrale [des Arts et Manufactures], once located at 5, rue de Thorigny (3rd)—he attended this school originally housed in the Hôtel Salé, which is now the Musée Picasso

- 1, rue Rabelais (8th)—longtime residence of Eiffel where he died at age ninety-one

- Bon Marché, 24, rue de Sèvres (7th)—the elegant department store, the first in France and the only one on the Left Bank, which Eiffel helped create

- Synagogue des Tournelles, 21 bis, rue des Tournelles (4th)— Eiffel's construction of this house of worship can be admired during free tours

- La Tour Eiffel, 5, avenue Anatole France (7th)—here's the address just in case you don't know where to find the imposing tower

Charles Garnier (1825-1898)

The "wow factor" of the mid-nineteenth-century Paris opera house is due in large part to the work of a myriad of craftsmen. But the initial design of the building sprang from the mind of one man: Charles Garnier. So how did the son of a poor Parisian family become the architect of such a marvel? Surprisingly, his success was a product of his sickly childhood. Garnier's mother refused to allow her frail son to follow in her husband's footsteps as a blacksmith. Instead, young Charles took courses in drawing and math before studying architecture at the famous École des Beaux-Arts. After Garnier received the fine arts school's Prix de Rome scholarship in 1848, he spent five years in the Italian capital where he was stirred by the splendor of Roman architecture. Once back home, Garnier witnessed the onset of Prefect Haussmann's renovations of Paris. As part of the vast urban renewal program, Emperor Napoléon III announced a competition for proposals to build the city's crowning glory, a new opera house. Over 170 designs were submitted and the 35-year-old Garnier was unanimously awarded the contract. An architect on the deciding jury spoke of his admiration for the "simplicity, clarity, logic, [and] grandeur" of Garnier's plans. The massive building with its splendid hall and grand marble staircase came in way over budget and took fourteen years to construct, having been slowed down by the effects of the Franco-Prussian War. Later, Garnier went on to design many buildings including the Grand Concert Hall of what is now called the Opéra de Monte-Carlo.

Addresses for Garnier

- 264, rue Mouffetard (5th)—the future architect was born into a working-class family on this now charming street

- École Gratuite de Dessin, 22, rue Saint-André-des-Arts (5th)— Garnier attended math and drawing classes at the school once found here

- École des Beaux-Arts, 14, rue Bonaparte (6th)—he then studied architecture at the prestigious fine arts school

- 90, boulevard Saint-Germain (5th)—Garnier and his wife Louise had an apartment at this address overlooking the Cluny Museum

- Opéra Garnier, place de l'Opéra (9th)—expert guided visits as well as self-tours are available to view Garnier's chef-d'œuvre

- Cimetière du Montparnasse, 3, boulevard Edgar Quinet (14th)— his grave is found in the 11th division of this cemetery

Hector Guimard (1867-1942)

While wandering around Paris, visitors might notice some unusually pretty "dragonfly entrances" of the métro. Well, those designs were created from the imagination of this renowned architect. Guimard had a difficult relationship with his parents, so at thirteen he left his native Lyon to move to the French capital. Five years later he began studies at a top art and design school, the École nationale supérieure des arts décoratifs. As a student, he received all kinds of awards and subsequently worked as a professor at the school for nine years. On a trip to Brussels in 1894 he was inspired by architect Victor Horta's Art Nouveau townhouse. Horta advised the younger man to "banish the flower" in favor of plant stalks as a means of developing his own style. In addition, Guimard's ideal of harmony and continuity led him to pursue interior decoration and furniture design as well. Both the Petit Palais and the Musée d'Orsay have fine examples of his home furnishings. To see more of his architectural creations other than subway entrances, you can take a tour without stepping out of the 16th arrondissement. If time is limited, though, go by and see his masterpiece, the Castel Beranger, dismissed as "deranged" by his contemporaries. As more angular, less decorative buildings became preferable in the 1920s, Guimard modified his style accordingly. In 1938 fear of impending war with the Nazis sent him and his wife Adeline into exile in the United States. Guimard was later buried in Hawthorne, New York.

Addresses for Guimard

- École nationale supérieure des arts décoratifs, 31, rue d'Ulm (5th)—school where Guimard began a three-year course of study in 1885; he later took a teaching job there

- École des Beaux-Arts, 14, rue Bonaparte (6th)—he continued his studies at this fine arts school but did not receive a diploma

- Porte Dauphine (16th)—this métro station at the western terminus of line 2 is the only original Guimard subway entrance remaining; the one in Montmartre at Abbesses (18th) on line 12 was moved from its earlier location at the Hôtel de Ville

- 34, rue Boileau (16th)—this mansion, dating from 1891, can be glimpsed behind metal gates and flowering wisteria in the spring

- 41, rue Chardon Lagache (16th)—the architecture at this address announces the beginning of his Art Nouveau style

- 39, boulevard Exelmans (16th)—Guimard redid the former studio of Jean-Baptiste Carpeaux at the request of the sculptor's widow in 1894

- Le Castel Beranger, 14, rue Jean de la Fontaine (16th)—the architect's chef-d'œuvre was built when he was still in his twenties; look for his signature there and at #17, 19, 21, and 60 on the same street

- 122, avenue Mozart (16th)—the house Guimard designed between 1909 and 1912 for his wealthy American wife and himself

- 11, rue François Millet (16th)—apartment building he created in 1910

- Petit Palais, avenue Winston Churchill (8th) and Musée d'Orsay, quai Anatole France (7th)—two museums holding Guimard furnishings

Georges-Eugène Haussmann (1809-1891)

Talk about a monumental job! Quite literally. Haussmann's selection as Prefect of Paris during Napoléon III's urban renewal certainly put a lot on his plate. Fortunately, the public administrator had the intelligence and ego equal to the task. A cabinet minister who interviewed him for the position felt that being "big, strong, vigorous, energetic, and at the same time clever and devious" were the perfect qualities to ward off critics and accomplish the vast project. Haussmann set about building a new reservoir and employed thousands of workers to install water pipes, develop the sewer system, and connect gas lines. New avenues helped improve the circulation of traffic. On top of it all, he had two train stations and the Hôtel-Dieu hospital built. All this flurry of activity did not come without harsh criticism. Haussmann was blasted for destroying part of the Jardin du Luxembourg to allow the new boulevard Raspail to pass through. At Napoléon III's request he completed four new parks: the Bois de Boulogne, the Bois de Vincennes, Parc des Buttes-Chaumont, and finally the Parc

Montsouris. Besides mounting costs, perhaps the greatest controversies stemmed from the destruction of historic areas and particularly for displacing as many as 350,000 Parisians. Still, an abundance of taste and style remains: the opulent Opéra Garnier, for sure, as well as the omnipresent cream-colored buildings along the boulevards. All in all, in seventeen years the prefect made the city healthier, less congested, and more grand. Haussmann's work resulted in the emperor awarding him the title "baron."

Addresses for Haussmann

- 53, rue du Faubourg-du-Roule (8th)—Haussmann was born at this address near the Arc de Triomphe which ironically was destroyed during his renovation of the city

- Lycée Condorcet, 8, rue du Havre (9th)—he went to this high school near the Gare Saint-Lazare

- Conservatoire de Paris, 209, rue Jean Jaurès (19th)—besides studying law, Haussmann, a talented musician, also took courses at the Paris Conservatory

- 12, rue Boissy-d'Anglas (8th)—he and his wife Octavie lived at this address near the place de la Concorde

- Cimetière du Père Lachaise, 16, rue du Repos (20th)—Haussmann's burial place is in the 4th division of this cemetery

Eugène Viollet-le-Duc (1814-1879)

Some of the most revered monuments in France—Notre-Dame de Paris, Mont-Saint-Michel, Carcassonne—were saved through the restoration efforts of this architect. Raised in a well-educated household, Viollet-le-Duc, interestingly, did not have a degree in any of the arts. Instead, he sketched constantly on his own. And, despite his parents' urging, he rejected "the sterility" of classes at the École des Beaux-Arts for internships in architectural offices. In 1840, because of family connections with Prosper Mérimée, an author serving as Inspector General of Historic Monuments, Viollet-le-Duc was asked to renovate the basilica at Vézelay, three hours from the capital. As would be the case throughout his career, certain modifications he implemented were highly criticized as not being "authentic;" however, in this case the changes kept the roof from collapsing at Vézelay. Other projects came fast and furious…Sainte-Chapelle, Mont-Saint-Michel, the Reims cathedral, and the fortress of Carcassonne. A twenty-five year restoration of Notre-Dame included replacing bells, statues, and stained-glass windows destroyed during the French Revolution. He also added gargoyles, chimeras, and a spire with his own face on the apostle Saint Thomas. At one time the medieval revival projects he was heading throughout the country numbered over twenty. His passion for this style, he explained this way: "when one has the good fortune to possess a national architecture, the best thing is to keep it." Heavily inspired by art critic John Ruskin, Viollet wrote a ten-volume dictionary of early French architecture which in turn influenced Louis Sullivan and Frank Lloyd Wright. His biggest disappointment came when he lost the bid for the Paris opera house to Charles Garnier.

Addresses for Viollet-le-Duc

- 1, rue Chabanais (2nd)—a memorial plaque marks the building where Viollet-le-Duc was born

- Lycée Condorcet, then called Collège Bourbon, 8, rue du Havre (9th)—he attended this secondary school

- École de Dessin, once found at 5, rue de l'École de Médecine (6th)—he taught for a while at this drawing school

- 68, rue Condorcet (9th)—the residence and studio that Viollet designed and built for himself and his wife

- École des Beaux-Arts, 14, rue Bonaparte (6th)—for a short time he became a professor of arts and aesthetics at the school he refused to attend. Faculty and students objected to the fact that he was unschooled in architecture and had for the most part only restored buildings.

Chapter 6

Artists and Sculptors

NAMED FOR ITS LOCATION in the Salon Carré of the Louvre, the Salon de Paris had been the official exhibition of academic art—painting, sculpture, lithographs, etc.—from graduates of the Académie des Beaux-Arts since 1667. Having works accepted at the Salon assured artists successful careers through government and private commissions. The opening night *vernissage* was a grand social event. But gradually the jury became increasingly conservative, snubbing anything that wasn't realistic and traditional. In 1863, responding to complaints that two-thirds of the pieces had been rejected, Napoléon III instituted the Salon des Refusés ("Exhibition of Rejects"). Each day the galleries were packed with over a thousand visitors, many ridiculing works from artists like Manet and Whistler. As of 1874, Impressionists began holding their own exhibits and in 1903 another group created its Salon d'Automne ("Fall Salon"). This chapter will focus on painters and sculptors, many of them those Impressionist, Post-Impressionist, and Fauve Salon "Rejects" we hold in high esteem today.

Paul Cézanne (1839-1906)

The artist from Aix-en-Provence Picasso called "my one and only master" received little recognition in his lifetime. Yet over a forty-six-year career, Cézanne persisted, producing over 900 oils and 400 watercolors. Like many men of the time, he was pressed into studying law by his father, a wealthy banker. In the end Cézanne rebelled, moving to Paris in 1861 where he reunited with his childhood friend Émile Zola. Disappointments soon followed: he failed the entrance exam to the École des Beaux-Arts and had his work repeatedly rejected by the Salon. While studying at a private academy, he met other artists including his mentor Camille Pissarro who influenced Cézanne's change to a lighter color palette. Cézanne dabbled in Impressionist painting for a time, exhibiting at two of their independent shows. But the messiness of Impressionism, he realized, wasn't structured or analytical enough to suit his taste. For Cézanne believed in simplifying objects to their geometric essentials, wanting to "treat nature in terms of the cylinder, the sphere, and the cone." His subjects encompassed at least 200 still lifes and forty-five paintings of his wife Hortense. An 1895 show devoted to his work by art dealer Ambroise Vollard made Cézanne the first important French artist to build his reputation through a commercial gallery rather than a public exhibition. Never entirely comfortable in the capital, he moved back to Provence for good in the early 1880s. Late in his career he began painting directly from life such as his eighty famous depictions of Mont Sainte-Victoire. Two years before his death the Salon d'automne had an entire room devoted to his works.

Addresses for Cézanne

- 7, rue des Feuillantines (5th)—for a while in 1862 he lived at this address before moving to 39, rue d'Enfer, now avenue du Général Leclerc (14th)

- Académie Suisse, 4, quai des Orfèvres (1st)—he met Pissarro, Monet, Sisley, and Renoir while studying at this academy, named for its founder not the country

- 22, rue Beautrellis (4th)—Cézanne had an apartment here 1865 and again in 1867

- 53, rue Notre-Dame-des-Champs (6th)—in 1868 Cézanne lived at this address with his wife before moving the following year to 5, rue de Chevreuse (6th), then in 1872 to 45, rue Jussieu (5th)

- 120, rue de Vaugirard (6th)—the couple was at this address with their son in 1874 and the next year at 15, quai d'Anjou (4th) on the Île Saint-Louis

- Café de Guerbois, 9, avenue de Clichy, once grande rue des Batignolles (18th)—Cézanne met with Impressionist artists at this café

- 35, boulevard des Capucines (9th)—in April 1874 he had three paintings in the first Impressionist exhibit at the home of Nadar, Félix Tournachon

- 67, rue de l'Ouest (14th)— Cézanne lived at this location in 1875 then at #32 from 1880 to 1885

- 17, rue Chaptal (9th)—he visited the salon of Nina de Villard where he met Manet and poets Mallarmé and Verlaine

- 6, rue Laffitte (9th)—Vollard devoted an entire show to Cézanne in 1895

Camille Claudel (1864-1943)

An art critic described Claudel as "A revolt against nature; a woman genius." In her era, it is true, female sculptors were quite revolutionary. From the start she seemed to have it all: wealthy parents, beauty, and an early gift for working with soil and stone. In Nogent-sur-Seine the girl's talent caught the attention of sculptor Alfred Boucher who convinced her father to send her to study in Paris. Her mother, although opposed to the idea, then moved with her three children to the capital. Boucher, who had taken on the teenager as a student, was leaving town and asked Auguste Rodin to manage his class. Attracted by her fiery temperament and extraordinary ability, Rodin soon had the nineteen-year-old Claudel collaborating with him—as his model, muse, and lover. Creating sculptures like *The Kiss*, he found her help indispensable, saying "I consult with her about everything." During their passionate ten-year liaison, the jealous young woman often exploded over Rodin's relationship with Rose, his longtime companion. Before ending their intimacy Claudel had at least one abortion and possibly even gave birth to children. Meanwhile, her sculptures received favorable recognition from the Salon and the Exposition Universelle, even though some found the sexual nature of her work virile and unseemly. Admirers included art dealers as well as Debussy, a possible lover, who kept a copy of her statue *The Waltz* on his desk for the rest of his life. In a fit of rage Claudel destroyed many of her pieces, leading to lifelong internment in a mental institution beginning in 1913. She was later buried in a communal grave.

Addresses for Claudel

- 135 bis, boulevard du Montparnasse (6ᵗʰ)—she, her mother, and siblings lived here from 1882 to 1886 before moving to 111, rue Notre-Dame-des-Champs (6ᵗʰ)

- Académie Colarossi, 10, rue de la Chaumière (6ᵗʰ)—because few big-name art schools were open to women at the time, Claudel studied at this former academy in 1882

- 117, rue Notre-Dame-des-Champs (6ᵗʰ)—she shared an atelier at this address with Jessie Lipscomb, a female British sculptor and friend

- 182, rue de l'Université (7ᵗʰ)—after meeting Rodin, she worked on pieces like "The Burghers of Calais" at his atelier in the former state marble warehouse beginning in 1884

- 31, boulevard de Port-Royal (13ᵗʰ)—from 1886 to 1892 she occasionally lived with her brother Paul, a well-known writer; a commemorative plaque marks the building

- 19, quai de Bourbon (4ᵗʰ)—a plaque is also found at this address on Île Saint-Louis where Claudel lived and worked mostly as a recluse from 1899 until her internment

- Musée Rodin, 79, rue de Varenne (7ᵗʰ)—this museum has a room dedicated to her work set up by Rodin in 1914

- Musée Camille Claudel, 10, rue Gustave Flaubert, Nogent-sur-Seine—this 2017 museum, an hour and a half drive southeast of Paris, has nearly forty-five works by the sculptor

Edgar Degas (1834-1917)

Denying that he was an Impressionist, this artist preferred the term realist, saying "no art was ever less spontaneous than mine." Yet like his contemporaries, Degas portrayed everyday topics through the use of color, heavier brushstrokes, and movement. Born to a moderately wealthy family, he dropped the aristocratic-seeming *de Gas* to return to the family's original surname. An early painter, by eighteen he had created a studio in the family home. After high school, at his father's urging, Degas began to study law; at the same time, however, he registered as a copyist at the Louvre and soon enrolled at the École des Beaux-Arts. For several years the young man traveled to Italy to learn about art and to do portraits of family members in Naples as well as to New Orleans to visit his brother. Many of Degas's paintings between 1865 and 1870 were accepted at the Salon before he rejected the rigidity of Academic art. Movement is a key element in much of his work: horses at the racetrack, for example, and ballet dancers, which sold well and make up more than half of his output. His sculpture of *The Little Dancer at Fourteen* (1881)—with real hair and clothing—was his most controversial piece. Degas is also famous for off-center works such as *L'Absinthe* (1876) which pictures two people sitting side by side in a café yet isolated in their own thoughts. A misanthropic bachelor, he became an increasingly unpopular figure. According to Renoir: "What a creature he was, that Degas! All his friends had to leave him." He died nearly blind at eighty-three.

Addresses for Degas

- 8, rue Saint-Georges (9ᵗʰ)—born to the de Gas family at this address, he lost his mother at age thirteen

- Lycée Louis-le-Grand, 123, rue Saint-Jacques (5ᵗʰ)—Degas attended this high school where he studied drawing

- 4, rue de Mondovi (1ˢᵗ)—the teenager set up his first studio in his father's apartment

61

- École des Beaux-Arts, 14, rue Bonaparte (6th)—in 1855 he entered this fine arts school

- 13, rue Victor-Massé, then the rue de Laval (9th)—from 1859 to 1872 he lived and worked at this address; between 1890 and 1912 he had a workshop in the attic at #37 on the same street

- 77, rue Blanche (9th)—in the spring of 1873 he moved here

- 50, rue Lepic (18th)—Degas also had an atelier at this location

- 6, boulevard de Clichy (18th)—he lived on the fifth floor from 1912 until his death five years later

- Cimetière de Montmartre, 20, avenue Rachel (18th)—burial place of Degas in division 4 of this cemetery

André Derain (1880-1954)

For Gertrude Stein, Derain was "the embodiment of the adventurous spirit...the Christopher Columbus of modern art." And he showed this brave attitude throughout his career—varying his materials as well as his style. At fifteen, growing up outside Paris, Derain began to paint on his own. While taking engineering classes in the capital, he studied art at a private academy. Four years after meeting Matisse, he joined the older artist in Collioure in 1905 where they developed the boldly colored paintings for that year's Salon d'automne. Despite being derisively dubbed *Fauves* ("Wild Beasts"), these works revolutionized twentieth century art. In 1906 gallery owner Ambroise Vollard sent Derain to London to paint subjects like the Thames and Tower Bridge. Those paintings became some of his most popular works prompting one critic to write that they "made London seem so fresh and yet remain quintessentially English." On that trip Derain discovered African art and began working in ceramics, wood and stone sculpture. Once an art dealer purchased his entire studio in Montmartre in 1907, the artist found financial stability and started experimenting with Cubism in addition to using more muted tones. He also designed book covers, made mechanical marionettes for the Ballets Russes, and created costumes and décors for thirteen ballets, two operas, and two plays. At the height of his success in the 1920s, Derain was awarded Pittsburgh's Carnegie Prize, insuring an international reputation—and allowing him to collect cars, châteaux, and women. An infantryman who served at the Somme, Verdun, and Chemin des Dames in WWI, Derain was courted by the Germans during the second conflict and was later ostracized as a collaborator.

Addresses for Derain

- Académie Julian, 31, rue du Dragon (6th)—Derain studied at this art school while enrolled in engineering classes

- Cité des Fusains, 22, rue Tourlaque (18th)—he had a studio near the Cimetière Montmartre from 1906 to 1910

- Le Bateau-Lavoir, 13, place Émile Goudeau (18th)—Derain met Picasso at this literary and artistic residence in 1907

- 13, rue Bonaparte (6th)—Derain settled at this address in 1910

- 27, rue de Fleurus (6th)—he and his wife Alice were frequent visitors at Gertrude Stein's Saturday night salons

- 5, rue Douanier-Rousseau (14th)—in 1929 Derain had a house built opposite Braque's

- 112, rue d'Assas (6th)—the atelier of his friend Léopold Levy where Derain painted

- 20, rue de Varenne (7th)—he rented an apartment at this address in 1941

Paul Gauguin (1848-1903)

This artist learned to love exotic places early. Fleeing the regime of Napoléon III, his parents took their two toddlers to Peru where they lived with his mother's relatives for six years. As a young man, Gauguin served in the Navy before settling into a bourgeois lifestyle as a stockbroker at La Bourse, Paris's Wall Street. Just after starting his job at twenty-five, he began painting and visiting art galleries. He achieved some success in 1876 when a landscape was accepted at the annual Salon. By 1883 Gauguin decided to quit his job and become a full-time artist although he was married with five children. Financially strapped, they moved to Copenhagen to live with his in-laws. Something had to give—and it turned out to be his family. The mid-1880s were marked by Gauguin's frequent changes of scene: in Paris he studied ceramics; in Bretagne he was inspired by the "savage, primitive quality" of the peasants; in Martinique he was motivated by the light; back in Bretagne, he transformed reality in his art using pure color and lack of perspective for emotional or symbolic purposes. In 1888 Gauguin spent nine tempestuous weeks living with Van Gogh in Arles. Three years later, wanting to flee Western civilization, he sold some of his works for passage to Tahiti. Many of Gauguin's finest paintings and wood sculptures date from his time in Polynesia, including his allegory "Where do we come from? What are we? Where are we going?" But he also became a sexual predator—impregnating and giving syphilis to teenaged lovers. Gauguin died at fifty-four in the Marquesas Islands where he is buried.

Addresses for Gauguin

- 56, rue Notre-Dame-de-Lorette (9th)—the historic plaque noting Gauguin's birthplace is somewhat hidden

- 15, rue de Bruyère (9th)—during his bachelor days, he lived at this address and met Impressionists including Camille Pissarro at nearby cafés

- 8, rue Carcel (15th)—he had his first studio in a third-floor apartment here

- 28, place Saint-Georges (9th)—Gauguin lived at this location with his wife Mette before moving to 30, rue de Chaillot (16th)

- 74, rue des Fourneaux, now the rue Falguière (15th)—in 1877 the family moved to the Impasse Fremin near this address

- 10, rue Cail (10th)—Gauguin's home with his son Clovis in the mid-1880s

- Hôtel Delambre, 35, rue Delambre (14th)—a plaque indicates that the artist lived at this hotel in 1891

- 8, rue de la Grande-Chaumière (6th)—Gauguin stayed here on a trip home from Tahiti in 1893

Édouard Manet (1832-1883)

More appropriately called "the father of Modernism" rather than "Impressionism," this artist had a rebellious streak when it came to his work. However, as one critic correctly noted, Manet wanted to be both revolutionary as well as accepted by classical institutions—at the same time. Although talented in drawing as a boy, his wealthy and influential family urged him to pursue a career in law or the military. After twice failing the entrance exam to the École Navale, Manet was allowed to follow his true love in the arts. Studying at the atelier of Thomas Couture, he often battled with his teacher, a proponent of traditional painting. When the 1859 Academic Salon refused Manet's *Absinthe Drinker*, Couture commented, "How can anyone paint something so ugly?" A true scandal erupted in 1863 when his huge painting *Déjeuner sur l'herbe*—picturing men in suits picnicking beside a naked woman and a nude bather—was presented at the Salon. Yet the controversy gave Manet a name in Paris. A couple of years later, his portrayal of the brazen, naked prostitute *Olympia* caused the artist such humiliation that he fled to Spain for a time. His contemporary subject matter notwithstanding, Manet's technique of bold brush strokes, implied shapes, and lack of perspective also shocked his contemporaries. Still, big-name admirers—authors Zola and Baudelaire, artists Monet, Renoir, and Cézanne—supported him. Manet remained true to his belief that "one must be of one's time and paint what one sees." About a decade before his death at fifty-one from untreated syphilis, the artist realized true success.

Addresses for Manet

- 5, rue Bonaparte, formerly rue des Petits-Augustins (6th)—a white plaque indicates the birthplace of Manet on the building's first floor

- Collège Rollin, 12, avenue Trudaine (9th)—he attended this school now the Lycée Jacques-Decour

- 69, rue de Clichy (9th)—family moved here when Manet was in his early twenties

- 23, rue Victor-Massé, then rue de Laval (9th)—he studied for six years at the atelier of Thomas Couture which Manet complained felt like "entering a tomb"

- rue Lavoisier (8th), rue de la Victoire (9th), rue de Douai (9th), and rue Guyot, now the rue Médéric (17th)—between 1856 and 1861 he set up studios on these streets (no numbers found)

- Galerie Martinet, 26, rue des Italiens (9th)—in the early 1860s he began showing paintings at this gallery

- 66, rue de Richelieu (2nd)—Manet also presented his engravings at Alfred Cadart's publishing house

- 34, boulevard des Batignolles (17th)—after their wedding in 1863, Manet and his wife moved here with their son and Manet's mother

- Café de Guerbois, 9, avenue de Clichy, once grande rue des Batignolles (18th)—Manet first frequented this former café in 1866 and was soon joined at evening gatherings by Monet, Renoir, and Degas among others to discuss painting

- 60, rue Mazarine (6th)—he had another atelier here

- 4, rue Saint-Petersbourg (8th)—Manet maintained a studio at this location from 1872 to 1878

- Café de la Nouvelle-Athènes, once found at 9, place Pigalle (9th)—he frequented this café with his artist friends

- 77, rue d'Amsterdam (8th)—he had a vast, luxurious studio here in 1879 and began getting more favorable criticism

- 39, rue Saint-Petersbourg (8th)—Manet died at this address after moving here from #49 on the same street

- Cimetière de Passy, 2, rue du Commandant-Schloesing (16th)—he is buried in the 4th division of this cemetery

Henri Matisse (1869-1954)

Beneath a conservative suit and serious demeanor was a man trying to curb his inborn unruliness and an artist about to revolutionize his profession. Born to a wealthy grain merchant near the Belgian border, Matisse studied law in Paris and became a court administrator back home. While recovering from appendicitis, he discovered "a kind of paradise" using art supplies. He returned to the capital in 1891 taking classes in painting and becoming a copyist at the Louvre. His palette remained dark and conventional for five more years, however, before he discovered the luminous paintings of Van Gogh. At the 1905 fall Salon Matisse and others like Dérain used bright, dissonant colors to express emotion, triggering the term *Fauves* ("Wild Beasts") by an art critic who complained that "a pot of paint has been flung in the face of the public." The sight of Matisse's *Woman with Hat* caused some viewers to claw at the painting with their fingernails. Fortunately for the artist's morale, Gertrude and Leo Stein purchased the work. Often invited to visit the Steins, Matisse was instrumental in initiating their Saturday evening get-togethers where he met Picasso, his lifelong friend and rival. By 1917 Matisse moved south and began traveling extensively. In the '30s he illustrated books by Mallarmé and James Joyce and was commissioned to do a mural in Philadelphia for Dr. Albert Barnes, a collector of his work. A decade later Matisse decorated a chapel in Vence near Nice. In his final years, bedridden, he created a new art form using paper and scissors, always living by his creed: "Creativity takes courage."

Addresses for Matisse

- 12, avenue du Maine (15th)—in his early days in Paris Matisse lived here often having boiled rice for dinner; he then moved on to a humid room at 350, rue Saint-Jacques (5th)

- Académie Julian, 31, rue du Dragon (6th)—he studied art at this academy as well as at the École des arts décoratifs at 31, rue d'Ulm (5th) in 1892 and sculpture with Antoine Bourdelle at 14, rue de la Grande-Chaumière (6th)

- 14, rue de la Rochefoucault (9th)—after passing the Beaux-Arts exam in 1895, Matisse attended the atelier of Gustave Moreau; the address is now the site of Moreau's museum

- 6, rue Laffitte (9th)—Matisse had an exhibit at the gallery of Ambroise Vollard in 1904

- 19, quai Saint-Michel (5th)—he lived at this address at various times; a memorial plaque is on the building

- 27, rue de Fleurus (6th)—Matisse first met Picasso at Gertrude Stein's Saturday night salon in 1906

- 84, rue de Sèvres (7th)—in the early 1900s he ran an art school in a rented space at a convent formerly found at this location; later his Académie Matisse was found at #56 on the same street and then at 31-33, boulevard des Invalides (7th), original address of the Hôtel Biron

- 132, boulevard du Montparnasse (14th)—in 1945 Matisse spent four months living here

Claude Monet (1840-1926)

Anyone visiting Monet's home in Giverny believes what he said: "Color is my day-long obsession, joy, and torment." For brilliant shades abound: the pink and green of the house, the bright yellow dining room, the outstanding blossoms in his gardens. During his youth in Normandy, he created charcoal caricatures until landscape artist Eugène Boudin had Monet try oil painting *en plein air*. After military service, Monet studied in Paris where he befriended Manet, Renoir, and Bazille. But their new style of painting fell flat with the Académie des Beaux-Arts which rejected them several times from its annual Salon. At the young artists' own exhibit, Monet's "Impression, rising sun" led a critic to dismiss it as Impressionism. And the label stuck. Naturally, early rejections and lack of income took a toll on

Monet and his wife, artist's model Camille Doncieux. They were so poor that creditors began seizing paintings to recoup what they were owed. Camille, who was quite sickly, died in 1879. Four years later, while passing by Giverny on a train, Monet noticed a property which he rented and eventually purchased. He built a studio, created a pond, and had flowers planted, giving precise instructions for gardeners. At age fifty-one Monet married Alice Hoschéde, his friend's ex-wife, but she also predeceased him. In later years, Monet underwent surgery for cataracts and died of lung cancer at age eight-six. At his burial in Giverny, his friend, politician Georges Clemenceau, replaced the black cloth on the coffin with a flowered one, saying: "No black for Monet."

Addresses for Monet

- 45, rue Laffitte (9th)—Oscar-Claude Monet was born on the fifth floor of this building

- Église Notre-Dame de Lorette, 18 bis, rue de Châteaudun (9th)—baby Oscar, as he was first called, was baptized in this ornate Catholic church but would later declare himself an atheist

- 6, rue de Furstenberg (6th)—in the mid-1860s Monet shared an apartment with artist Frédéric Bazille at his address; later the two friends found quarters at 20, rue Visconti (6th)

- 35, boulevard des Capucines (9th)—the first Impressionist exhibit was held at the home of Felix Tournachon (known as Nadar) from mid-April to mid-May 1874; four oils and seven pastels from Monet were on display

- 20, rue Visconti (6th)—Monet found lodging in Bazille's apartment

- 26, rue d'Edimbourg (8th)—Monet and his wife lived here for a short while in 1878 where their second son was born

- 251, rue Saint-Honoré (1st)—thirty-five of his works were shown in 1882 at the Exposition des Artistes Indépendants

- 35, rue de Rome (8th)—he spent years decorating the sitting room of art dealer Paul Durand-Ruel

- 8, rue de Sèze (9th)—for the first time Monet participated in an international exhibition in 1885

- Musée Marmottan Monet, 2, rue Boilly (16th)—this museum has the largest collection of Monet paintings in the world (read more about it in Chapter 3)

- Musée d'Orsay, 5, quai Anatole France (7th)—eighty-six of his works are found here

Berthe Morisot (1841-1895)

Here's a real pioneer for you: the first female Impressionist artist. Ironically perhaps, as was often true for women in the past, Morisot wouldn't have succeeded without the support of the men in her life. Her affluent family, arriving in Paris from Bourges in 1852, made sure their young daughters took art lessons. Joseph Guichard, an early teacher, spoke highly of the girls' talents, prompting their father to build them a studio behind their house. Another male advocate was artist Édouard Manet who approved of Morisot's paintings as well as her beauty, having her pose for him a dozen times. Finally, her husband Eugène, Manet's brother, encouraged her to keep painting using her maiden name. And paint she did. Having family and friends as models, she portrayed domestic scenes from her bourgeois milieu. Tepid compliments from critics about her works having "feminine charm" didn't discourage the strong-willed Morisot. Instead, she realized her struggle in a masculine world: "I don't think there has ever been a man who treated a woman as an equal." Beginning in 1864, however, her paintings were accepted seven times at the Academic Salon. Ten years later she became the only woman in the first Impressionist exhibit, admired by fellow artists as a "virtuoso colorist." Her most famous work *The Cradle* (1872) shows Morisot's ability to use white to indicate transparency; that same year art dealer Paul Durand-Ruel bought twenty-two of her paintings. At an 1880 exhibition Morisot was judged one of the best Impressionist artists. Speculation about the cause of her early death ranges from pneumonia to the pulmonary syphilis that caused the death of her husband.

Addresses for Morisot

- 16, rue [Benjamin-] Franklin—the Morisot family lived here from 1865 to 1872 when they moved to 7, rue Guichard (both in the 16th)

- rue de Lille, (7th)—because art classes were approved for girls of the time, she and her sister began studying with painter Geoffroy-Alphonse Chocarne in his atelier (no number found); then with Joseph Guichard, 35, rue des Moulins (1st)

- Notre-Dame-de-Grâce-de-Passy, 8 bis, rue de l'Annonciation (16th)—Morisot married Eugène Manet in this church on December 22, 1874

- 35, boulevard des Capucines (9th)—she was the only woman presenting at the first Impressionist exhibit in the home of Felix Tournachon (Nadar) from mid-April to mid-May 1874

- 9, avenue d'Eylau, now avenue Victor-Hugo (16th)—the couple had an apartment here in 1876

- 40, rue Villejuste, now rue Paul Valéry, (16th)—in 1883 she, her husband, and daughter Julie moved into their extravagant, newly-built home close to the Arc de Triomphe; a memorial plaque is on the building

- 11, rue le Peletier (9th)—she participated in the second and third Impressionist shows at the gallery of Paul Durand-Ruel; a retrospective of her works was held here the year after her death

- 10, rue Weber (16th)—residence and atelier of Morisot after her husband died in 1892

- Cimetière de Passy, 2, rue du Commandant Scholesing (16th)—Morisot is buried next to her husband and brother-in-law in this cemetery

Pierre-Auguste Renoir (1841-1919)

According to Renoir: "Art is about emotion. If art needs to be explained, it is no longer art." This principle helped him create thousands of works which evoke warm sensuality through light and color. A few years after his birth in central city of Limoges, the family moved, fittingly enough, to an apartment near the Louvre in Paris. The boy showed an early talent for drawing but was so accomplished as a singer that he took classes with French composer Charles Gounod. At thirteen, Renoir had a successful apprenticeship painting on porcelain at a factory near the Marais. Frequent trips to the Louvre inspired him to begin studies at the École des Beaux-Arts. Some of his first paintings were accepted by the jury of the state-sponsored Académie for their annual Salon. Subsequent rejections by the Academy, however, led to Renoir's associating with Impressionist friends, adopting their approach, and taking part in their alternative exhibits. Throughout his career, however, the artist had a tendency to vary his style between Impressionism and Classicism. In 1890 he married his longtime model Aline Charigot, who is pictured holding a small dog in Renoir's famous *Luncheon of the Boating Party*. (Which, by the way, sold for a hefty $78 million in 1990.) The couple's three sons were also quite talented—an actor, a ceramic artist, and filmmaker Jean Renoir (see Chapter 4). Once he developed rheumatoid arthritis, Renoir moved to the South of France near Nice and, despite the pain, continued to paint for the rest of his life.

Addresses for Renoir

- 23, rue d'Argenteuil (1st)—early location of the Renoir family apartment

- École des Beaux-Arts, 14, rue Bonaparte (6th)—in 1862 at age twenty he entered this famous fine arts school

- 9, rue de la Condamine, the number has disappeared (17th)— Renoir shared a room with Frédéric Bazille, who was richer than the other artists, at this address and also at 20, rue Visconti and at 8, rue des Beaux-Arts (both in the 6ᵗʰ)

- Café Guerbois, formerly found at 9, avenue de Clichy (18ᵗʰ)—a gathering place for artists, the old name of this street, grande rue des Batignolles, gave some of the young Impressionists their initial name: le Groupe des Batignolles

- 35, rue Saint-Georges (9ᵗʰ)—Renoir had a studio here when he met his future wife Aline

- 35, boulevard des Capucines (9ᵗʰ)—the artist presented six paintings in the first Impressionist exhibit at the home of Felix Tournachon (Nadar) from mid-April to mid-May 1874

- 12, rue Cortot (18ᵗʰ)—[the current location of the Musée de Montmartre] Renoir rented a space at this address to create "Bal du moulin de la Galette;" the dance hall that served as his inspiration was at that time situated at 79, rue Lepic (18ᵗʰ) five minutes away

- 11, rue le Peletier (9ᵗʰ)—he participated in the second Impressionist exhibit at the gallery of Paul Durand-Ruel

- 13, rue Taitbout (9ᵗʰ)—the first exhibit devoted entirely to Renoir was held here; Durand-Ruel would later have another Renoir showing at 9, boulevard de la Madeleine (1ˢᵗ)

- Cité des Artistes, 24, rue Norvins (18ᵗʰ)—Renoir found inspiration at this art colony, still in operation

- 37, rue de Laval, now Victor Massé (9ᵗʰ)—he and his wife lived at this address and in 1884 moved to 18, rue Houdon (18ᵗʰ) where their first son Pierre was born

- 11, boulevard de Clichy (9ᵗʰ)—from 1909 to 1911 Renoir had a studio here

Auguste Rodin (1840-1917)

This sculptor of *The Thinker* gained notoriety before becoming famous. His life-sized male figure entitled *L'Âge d'airain* was so realistic that critics accused him of having cheated by using the mold of a real man. Lesson learned: Rodin's later sculptures were purposely larger or smaller than life. He first got interested in drawing at the age of ten. But a few years later as a student at the Petite École, he was introduced to modeling clay and felt he had "mounted up to the heavens." Deciding to become a sculptor, Rodin tried to get accepted into the École des Beaux-Arts but failed the entrance exam three times. Meanwhile, he studied with other artists and took jobs as a craftsman—fashioning decorative objects and architectural additions to buildings during Haussmann's renovation of Paris. In the early 1870s Rodin gained more skill and experience by working on the Belgian stock exchange building in Brussels. On tour of Italy in 1875 he discovered Michelangelo who "freed me from academic sculpture." This epiphany led to the creation of *The Age of Bronze*—the statue first believed to be a fraud. Back in Paris and working as a professor of art in 1882, he met a gifted, teenaged student named Camille Claudel who became his assistant, muse, model, and lover. After fifteen years living in Meudon, the sculptor returned to Paris in 1908, making his home in the Hôtel Biron, future site of the Musée Rodin. Before dying from pneumonia at age seventy-seven, he married Rose Beuret, his faithful companion for fifty-three years.

Addresses for Rodin

- 3, rue de l'Arbalète (5ᵗʰ)—Rodin was born here
- 12, rue des Fossés-Saint-Jacques (5ᵗʰ)—for three years the family lived at this address before moving to #6 on the same street and then on to 91, rue de la Tombe Issoire (14ᵗʰ)
- École des arts décoratifs, 5, rue École de la Médecine (6ᵗʰ)—he attended the so-called Petite École from ages fourteen to seventeen
- 23, rue de la Reine Blanche (13ᵗʰ)—in 1863 the young Rodin got his own apartment
- 175, rue Marcadet (18ᵗʰ)—before leaving for Brussels he and Rose lived here

- 3, rue des Bretonvilliers (4ᵗʰ)— on their return to Paris in 1877 the couple had an apartment on the Île St. Louis

- 182, rue de l'Université (7ᵗʰ)—after the state purchased one of his sculptures in 1882, Rodin was granted an atelier at the former marble warehouse

- 268, rue Saint-Jacques (5ᵗʰ)—from 1877 to 1882 he created his monumental *La Porte de l'Enfer* (*Gates of Hell*) at this workshop

- 10, rue de la Grande Chaumière (6ᵗʰ)—as a teacher at the former art academy at this address, Rodin met Camille Claudel in 1882

- 71, rue de Bourgogne (7ᵗʰ)—between 1884 and 1890 the sculptor lived here

- 23, rue des Grands Augustins (6ᵗʰ)—he spent two years at this location

- 79, rue de Varenne (7ᵗʰ)—in 1908 Rodin found an old mansion about to be torn down and made it into his workshop and eventually his museum

Henri de Toulouse-Lautrec (1864-1901)

Through paintings and sketches of dancers, lesbians, and prostitutes this artist came to embody Montmartre. So how did a young aristocrat manage to treat such subjects with kindness and sensitivity? The answer is that, like them, Lautrec felt an outsider. Brittle bones due to family inbreeding caused deformations of his legs and he suffered greatly from the taunts of others because of his normal-sized torso on a four feet, eight inches frame. When his parents split up, the mother and eight-year-old son left the southwestern town of Albi for Paris. Drawings he made all over his notebooks showed promise and led to taking art classes. Through his academic teachers Lautrec learned the basics, met fellow students like Van Gogh, and, thanks to their ateliers' location, discovered a new, bohemian part of town. Lautrec then immersed himself in the cabarets and brothels of Montmartre, producing elegant and sometimes provocative images of local women in various poses: at rest, bathing, combing their hair, or putting on makeup. Inspired by Manet and Degas, Lautrec developed a style all his own. Because of the invention of the lithograph, he was able to create iconic publicity posters for dancers like La Goulue and Jane Avril as well as for singer Aristide Bruant. Frequent mocking of his appearance drove him to drink to excess, including a powerful combination of absinthe and brandy called *Tremblement de terre* ("Earthquake"). Lautrec spent three months for detox in a sanatorium in Neuilly where he produced thirty-nine circus portraits from memory. After a series of serious medical issues, Lautrec died of alcoholism and syphilis at age thirty-six.

Addresses for Toulouse-Lautrec

- Lycée Condorcet, then called the Lycée Fontanes, 8, rue du Havre (9th)—he attended this high school where he failed the *bac* in 1881

- 233, rue du Faubourg Saint-Honoré (8th)— Lautrec lived for a while with his first art teacher René Princeteau

- 30, rue de Clichy (9th)—he appreciated classes with portraitist Léon Bonnat who often criticized Lautrec's drawings as "quite simply atrocious"

- 10, rue Constance and later at 104, boulevard de Clichy (both in the 18th)—Lautrec studied for five years with Beaux-Arts teacher Fernand Cormon and met fellow students Vincent Van Gogh and Albert René Grenier

- 5, rue Tourlaque (18th)—he shared a third-floor studio with artist Suzanne Valadon

- 19 bis, rue Pierre-Fontaine (9th)—in June 1884 Lautrec moved into the vast apartment of Grenier whose sister Lily, Lautrec's model, lived in the same building

- Le Chat Noir, 84, boulevard Rochechouart (18th)—he created posters for Rodolphe Salis's famous cabaret which later moved to 12, rue de Laval, now rue Victor-Massé, (9th) and then to 68, boulevard de Clichy (18th)

- Le Mirliton, 84, boulevard Rochechouart (18th)—after Le Chat Noir moved out of this site, Aristide Bruant set up his own cabaret, one of Lautrec's favorites

- Moulin Rouge, 82, boulevard Clichy (18th)—when this cabaret opened, Lautrec was commissioned to do a series of posters for La Goulue which assured him a front row seat

- 21 (or possibly #27), rue Caulaincourt (18th)—he had an atelier above his father's apartment from 1887 to 1893 where he lived with med student Henri Bourges

- 21, rue Pierre-Fontaine (9th)—he had an apartment on the left side of the third floor from 1891 to 1893

- 9, rue de Douai (9th)—he and friends often had dinner with Lautrec's mother at this address

- 8, rue d'Amboise (2nd)—now a three-star hotel, a plaque marks this former house of prostitution where Lautrec lived from time to time and left his drawings of the women

- Folie Saint-James, 16, avenue de Madrid, Neuilly—in 1899 Lautrec was interned for alcohol detox treatment in this sanatorium near the Bois de Boulogne

- 15, avenue Frochot (9th)—from 1898 until his death he had an atelier here and lived down the street at #5

- Musée de Montmartre, 12, rue Cortot (18th)—this museum contains a fine collection of the artist's works

Chapter 7

Authors

When it comes to producing fine literature, French writers are hard to beat. Members of the Nobel committee evidently agree, having awarded their annual literary prize to more French authors than to any other nationality. In addition, many other excellent, well-known novelists, playwrights, poets, and short story writers who have not been recognized as Nobel laureates are worthy of exploring…which makes choices for this section particularly difficult. In addition to the requirement that they lived for a time in Paris, I've also decided to focus on those who achieved international fame in the 19th and 20th centuries. Beginning with the eldest of the group, Balzac (born 1799), this chapter contains such important names as Hugo, Flaubert, Proust, Sand, Verne, and Zola. As always, I hope reading about these authors will encourage you to discover and enjoy some of their works.

Honoré de Balzac (1799-1850)

At this author's funeral Victor Hugo described "a nation in mourning for a man of genius." And a genius Balzac was. For he shared his brilliant insights into human nature in a vast number of works. The family name, adopted by his father, was chosen to eliminate what he considered the peasant connotations of Balssa. (In keeping with this tradition, the author later added the aristocratic particle "de" to be more accepted by high society.) A willful child, Balzac hated the rote learning in boarding school. In 1814 the family left Tours for Paris where the teenaged Honoré attended the Sorbonne. At twenty, after failing at several occupations, he decided to become a writer. Living in a garret in the capital, he churned out nine potboilers in seven years. In 1832 Balzac conceived of a sequence of novels which would become his greatest achievement: *La Comédie Humaine.* His plan was to combine previous and new works to portray "all aspects of society." Balzac's keen observation helped him invent complex, fully human social types...such as those in best sellers like *Eugénie Grandet* (1833) and *Père Goriot* (1835). Adding to the realism, the author incorporated details of their clothing, possessions, and décor, sometimes having characters recur in other novels. Fueled by coffee, he maintained harmful work habits; writing all night—sometimes for fifteen hours straight—while obsessively revising. A fan letter he received from a Polish countess in Russia initiated a fifteen-year correspondence. By the time of their marriage, however, Balzac's health had so deteriorated that he died five months later, his magnum opus well-developed but unfinished.

Addresses for Balzac

- Le Procope, 13, rue de l'Ancienne-Comédie (6th)—Balzac frequented this café, the oldest in Paris

- 17, rue Visconti (6th)—working as a printer, he set up a shop at this address from 1826 to 1828; a plaque is located here

- 6, rue Bonaparte (6th)—another memorial plaque honoring Balzac's novel *César Birotteau* is on this building

- 7, rue des Grands Augustins (6th)—the author situated the action of his short story *Le Chef-d'œuvre inconnu* at this address

- 47, rue Raynouard (16th)—for seven years Balzac lived in this house where he wrote and revised *La Comédie humaine*; it's now a free museum dedicated to him (see Chapter 3)

- 136, boulevard Raspail (6th)—at the place Pablo-Picasso stands a statue of Balzac by Rodin

- Cimetière du Père Lachaise, 16, rue du Repos (20th)—a David d'Angers bust marks Balzac's grave in division 48 of this cemetery

Charles Baudelaire (1821-1867)

How, one wonders, could lyric poetry cause such a furor? When *The Flowers of Evil* appeared in 1857, readers were aghast at its themes of sex and death. The government took legal action against the poet, his editor, and the printer for immorality. But the thirty-six-year-old Baudelaire was used to being a rebel. When his mother remarried a year after losing her husband, the young boy revolted. In high school he adopted a bohemian lifestyle, frequenting prostitutes and spending exorbitantly. Trying to curb the boy's unconventional ways, his family sent him on a boat to the Far East. He got as far as Reunion Island before heading home, unchanged except for a desire to write poetry. Once he used up half the inheritance from his father, Baudelaire was legally constrained by a trust which he deeply resented. Around that time, he had a series of mistresses, beginning with the mixed-race Jeanne Duval who unsurprisingly was rejected by his conservative family. To earn a living at twenty-four he became an art critic and a journalist. By 1847 Baudelaire discovered an affinity with Poe, translating many of his works. As is often the case, the controversy engendered by the obscenity trial made *Les Fleurs du mal* popular. A second edition, minus six deleted poems, was issued in 1861. To escape creditors the author moved to Belgium in the mid-1860s where he continued using opium and began drinking to excess. Baudelaire, already syphilitic, suffered a massive stroke, dying a year later in Paris. For Symbolist poets like Rimbaud, their precursor Baudelaire was "a true God."

Addresses for Baudelaire

- 13, rue Hautefeuille (6th)—his birthplace is marked with a memorial plaque

- Église Saint-Sulpice, 2, rue Palatine (6th)—Baudelaire was baptized in this church

- Lycée Louis-le-Grand, 123, rue Saint-Jacques (5th)—after boarding school in Lyon, he attended this high school, was dismissed in 1839, but somehow earned his degree

- La Tour d'Argent, 15, quai de la Tournelle (5th)—this historic, extravagant restaurant was a favorite of the author (read more about it in Chapter 2)

- 22, quai de Béthune, then #10 (4th)—at twenty-one Baudelaire had his first studio on the Île Saint-Louis from 1842 to 1843; a plaque marks the building

- Hôtel de Lauzun, then the Hôtel Pimodan, 17, quai d'Anjou (4th)—he wrote *Les Fleurs du Mal* when he lived on the fourth floor at this address; between 1844 and 1849 he and friends Dumas, Hugo, Balzac, and Delacroix experimented with hashish and opium at this mansion now a museum

- 1, rue du Dôme (16th)—from the summer 1866 until his death a year later Baudelaire, in a half-paralyzed state, was cared for at a clinic at this address where Manet and his wife often visited him

- Cimetière du Montparnasse, 3, boulevard Edgar Quinet (14th)—Baudelaire is interred in division 6 this cemetery; there is also a monument devoted to him between divisions 26 and 27

Simone de Beauvoir (1908-1986)

In *The Second Sex*, her groundbreaking work of 1949, Beauvoir describes, in part, the masculine world and the "myths concocted by men" which influenced her childhood. This nearly one thousand-page book was instrumental in laying the foundation for modern feminism. True to her anti-bourgeois philosophy, Beauvoir embraced a lifestyle of what she considered freedom: saying "non" to marriage, children, and permanent lodging. Instead, she led a life of sexual liberty, adopting a female lover as her child near the end of her life, and, for a long while, living a quasi-nomadic existence moving from hotel to hotel. A native Parisian and a brilliant student, Beauvoir was schooled in the city, acquiring a degree in philosophy at the Sorbonne in 1927. Two years later she placed second to Jean-Paul Sartre on the *agrégation*, a final exam which certifies candidates to teach on the secondary or university level. The couple's initial meeting led to a fifty-year "open relationship" where they frankly discussed their sexual escapades with each other. They even shared female partners, many of them their own students. After Beauvoir was dismissed from teaching in 1943, she turned her full attention to writing. While she enjoyed sitting by the Médicis fountain at the Luxembourg Gardens, most of her time was spent writing in the grand cafés of Saint-Germain. A prolific author, Beauvoir produced short stories, novels, essays, articles for a leftist journal *Les Temps modernes* which she helped found, in addition to a multi-volume autobiography. She is buried next to Sartre in Montparnasse cemetery.

Addresses for Beauvoir

- La Rotonde, 105, boulevard du Montparnasse (6th)—Beauvoir was born in an apartment over this well-known restaurant

- 71, rue de Rennes (6th)—financial troubles forced the family to downsize a short distance away in 1919

- Institut Normal Catholique Adéline Désir, 41, rue Jacob (6th)—until she was seventeen, Beauvoir attended this girls' school

- Institut catholique de Paris, 21, rue d'Assas (6th)—Beauvoir studied math at the Catholic university

- École normale supérieure, 45, rue d'Ulm (5th)—she sat in classes and took the agrégation exam at this very selective graduate school

- 91, avenue Denfert-Rochereau (14th)—from 1929 to 1931, to get away from her mother, Beauvoir lived in a studio belonging to her grandmother

- Hôtel Royal-Bretagne, 11 bis, avenue de la Gaité—for one year she had a room at this hotel, often having breakfast at Le Dôme, 108, boulevard du Montparnasse, a short walk away (both in the 14th)

- Hôtel des Bains, 33, rue Delambre—in the spring of '37 she stayed at this hotel, moving in the fall for a two-year stay at the Hôtel Mistral, 24, rue Cels (both in the 14th); a plaque marks the second building

- Hôtel Danemark, 21, rue Vavin (6th)—Beauvoir lived here on two different occasions

- Le Tabou, 33, rue Dauphine (6th)—she enjoyed a gin fizz at this club once found in the basement of the Hôtel d'Aubusson, still at this address, where she had a room in the early '40s

- Hôtel La Louisiane, 60, rue de Seine (6th)—for several years Beauvoir lived in room 68 on the top floor of this hotel

- 11, rue de la Bûcherie (5th)—from 1948 to 1955 she lived here where she wrote *The Second Sex* and *The Mandarins*; the latter, a novel, was awarded the Prix Goncourt

- Les Deux Magots, 6, place Saint-Germain-des-Prés and the Café de Flore, 172, boulevard Saint-Germain-des-Prés (next to each other in the 6th)—two favorite writing spots of Beauvoir and Sartre along with other members of the literary élite of the period

- 11 bis, rue Schoelcher (14th)—a white plaque marks the building where she lived on the ground floor from 1955 until her death in 1986

- Cimetière du Montparnasse, 3, boulevard Edgar Quinet (14th)— Beauvoir is buried in the 20th division of this cemetery

- La Passerelle Simone de Beauvoir, between the pont de Bercy and the pont de Tolbiac—true fans might want to visit the newest bridge in Paris named for the writer

Albert Camus (1913-1960)

If you read *The Stranger* in high school, you are already somewhat familiar with Camus. A "pied-noir" (French national born in colonial Algeria), he was raised in poverty by his mother and grandmother after his father died during World War I. Through the efforts of a teacher, he got a scholarship to a good secondary school near Algiers where he studied philosophy. After college in 1940, a friend found him a job at a newspaper in Paris and introduced him to others including his idol, author André Malraux. Three years later he began a friendship with Sartre and Beauvoir which ended over Camus's rejection of Russian totalitarianism. A cultural outsider, he never really felt comfortable in the capital though the Gallimard family provided emotional and some financial support when he worked for their press. After the Second World War began, Camus, unable to join the army because of a history of tuberculosis, became involved in the Resistance as editor-in-chief of an underground paper *Le Combat*. Some of his plays of the period served as the basis for future novels. *The Plague* (1947), his greatest success, sold hundreds of thousands of copies worldwide. Though married, Camus engaged in countless affairs; the love of his life, however, was undoubtedly Spanish actress Maria Casarès. A few years before his death, the author was awarded the Nobel Prize for his literary production whose "earnestness illuminates the problems of human conscience in our times." The brilliant author, philosopher, and Resistance member died tragically in an automobile accident at age forty-six. He's buried in the southern town of Loumarin.

Addresses for Camus

- Hôtel du Poirier, 16, rue Ravignan (18th)—from March to May 1940 Camus stayed in this former hotel in Montmartre where he finished writing a draft of *L'Étranger*

- Hôtel Madison, 143, boulevard Saint-Germain (6th)—in June 1940 he switched to better accommodations here

- Paris-Soir, 37, rue du Louvre (2nd)—location of the former newspaper where Camus first worked through the efforts of his friend Pascal Pia

- 100, rue Réaumur (2nd)—*Le Combat* newspaper was headquartered here after the Liberation of Paris

- 1 bis, rue Vaneau (7th)—in October '44 he and his wife Francine spent some time here in André Gide's apartment

- 148, rue de Vaugirard (15th)—Camus often met his mistress Maria Casarès at Gide's apartment or at hers at this address

- Café de Flore, 172, boulevard Saint-Germain (6th)—a hangout for Beauvoir, Sartre, and Camus

- 67, rue Monsieur le Prince (6th)—once the location of the Le Hoggar, the author's favorite café for couscous, now a cinema multiplex

- 5, rue Gaston Gallimard, once rue Sébastien-Bottin (7th)—address of Camus's publisher where he also worked as a selection reader

- 18, rue Seguier (6th)—after living in Vincennes, in December 1946 the author, his wife, and twins spent nearly four years in this apartment belonging to the Gallimards

- Théâtre Hébertot, 78 bis, boulevard des Batignolles (17th)—Maria Casarès starred in a production of Camus's play *Les Justes* at this theater in 1950

- 29, rue Madame (6th)—that same year Camus bought a five-room apartment for his family at this address

- Café de la Mairie, 8, place Saint-Sulpice (6th)—the author used to have coffee and read the papers every morning here

[Sidonie-Gabrielle] Colette (1873-1954)

Scandal surrounded this author's life and work. But despite it all, Colette was cherished by the public and received both critical and commercial acclaim for her writings. Her happy childhood in Burgundy, about two hours southeast of Paris, was spent reading the classics and learning the art of observation from her mother. Life changed drastically at twenty when she married a Parisian womanizer, the music critic/journalist called Willy. Her husband, who also produced ghost-written popular novels, asked her to write down her childhood memories. The resulting novel *Claudine at School*—published under his name in 1900—took Paris by storm, leading to a book series and launching products such as face powder and cigarettes. After leaving Willy in 1906, Colette had some lean times. During a six-year music hall career, she performed risqué skits, once nearly causing a riot by kissing another woman on stage at the Moulin Rouge. In 1912 Colette married another journalist and gave birth to a daughter. The five-year intimate relationship she had with her sixteen-year-old stepson led to her novel *Chéri* (1920). That book and *Gigi* (1944), probably her most famous works, were both adapted to the big screen. During her lifetime Colette received high praise from authors like Katherine Anne Porter who called her "the greatest living French writer." She was elected Grand Officer of Légion d'honneur, was admitted to the literary circle Académie Goncourt, and was nominated for the Nobel Prize in Literature in 1948. After her death at age eighty-one, Colette became the first French woman of letters accorded a state funeral.

Addresses for Colette

- 28, rue Jacob (6ᵗʰ)—a plaque marks the building where Colette and Willy lived in a dilapidated attic from 1893 to 1896—after spending a few weeks above his family's publishing business at 55, quai des Grands Augustins (6ᵗʰ)

- 93, rue de Courcelles (8ᵗʰ)—the couple moved to this address in 1901 followed by another apartment at #177 bis on the same street the next year

- 44, rue Villejust, now the rue Paul Valéry (16ᵗʰ)—Colette lived here alone after splitting with Willy but often stayed with her lover, the French marquise known as Missy at 2, rue Georges-Ville (also in the 16ᵗʰ)

- Moulin Rouge, 82, boulevard de Clichy (18ᵗʰ)—in a skit at this music hall called *Rêve d'Égypte* (*Egyptian Dream*) Colette kissed Missy on stage causing a near riot

- 57, rue Cortambert (16ᵗʰ)—she moved in with Henry de Jouvenel here before relocating to 62, boulevard Suchet (16ᵗʰ) in 1917

- 9, rue de Beaujolais (1ˢᵗ)—Colette made her home on the mezzanine of this building from 1927 to 1930 and again on the second floor, Palais-Royal side, from 1938 until her death; you can still see her letter C intertwined with the sun on the balcony; a commemorative plaque is also found here

- (Fraser Suites) Le Claridge, 74, avenue des Champs-Élysées (8ᵗʰ)—she had an apartment at this hotel in the early '30s

- 6, rue de Miromesnil (8ᵗʰ)—at this address in 1932 Colette opened a short-lived beauty institute selling cosmetics and perfumes

- Le Grand Véfour, 17, rue de Beaujolais (1ˢᵗ)—a gold nameplate marks her favorite seat at this fine restaurant where Julia Child wrote about seeing Colette's "fierce visage and a wild tangle of gray hair"

- Cimetière du Père Lachaise, 16, rue du Repos (20ᵗʰ)—she is interred in division 4 near the main entrance of the cemetery

Alphonse Daudet (1840-1897)

Anyone who has ever read *Letters from my Windmill* will undoubtedly agree with Émile Zola about the "profound charm" of Daudet's works. As the child of Catholic, royalist parents in the southern city of Nîmes, he developed a "habit to record life" early on. After moving the family to Lyon, the father, a silk merchant, endured financial ruin, prompting sixteen-year-old Alphonse to take a position as a teacher near his hometown. That painful experience he would later document in his semi-autobiographical novel *Le Petit Chose* ("Little Whatchamacallit"). In 1857 Daudet abandoned teaching and moved in with his brother in Paris. His joyful bohemian life in the capital had a dark side: he contracted syphilis which would cause him great suffering at the end of his life. While working as a journalist for the *Figaro* and other newspapers, Daudet published a small volume of poetry in 1858. Around the same time he met Frédéric Mistral, a successful Provençal author. That encounter gave Daudet the idea of exaggerating his links with Provence to advance his career. For five years he served as the secretary to the Duc de Morny, a minister and stepbrother of Napoléon III. Once the duke died in 1865, Daudet became a full-time writer, often working in collaboration with others. A trip to Provence inspired the popular short stories of *Lettres de mon moulin*, published as a series by the newspaper *L'Événement* in the summer of 1866. In spite of his close friendship with Zola, Daudet was firmly against Dreyfus and supported anti-Jewish groups. He died at age fifty-seven of neurosyphilis which had affected his spinal cord.

Addresses for Daudet

- Odéon Théâtre de l'Europe, formerly Théâtre national de l'Odéon, 1, place de l'Odéon (6th)— Daudet's play *La Dernière Idole* (written in collaboration) was staged at this theater in the early 1860s

- Hôtel de Lamoignon, 24, rue Pavée (4th)—from 1867 to 1873 he lived here

- 31, rue de Bellechasse (7th)—a commemorative plaque marks this building where the author resided with his family from 1885 to 1897 until poor health prevented him from climbing to the fifth floor

- 41, rue de l'Université (7th)—he died in his first-floor apartment where a second plaque can be found

- Cimetière du Père Lachaise, 16, rue du Repos (20th)—Daudet is buried in the 26th division of this cemetery; Émile Zola delivered the eulogy at his funeral

Alexandre Dumas, père (1802-1870)

Dumas Davy de la Pailleterie had the somewhat unusual heritage of being a mixed-race aristocrat. Like his father, he took the name Dumas from his grandmother, a black slave in Saint-Domingue, present-day Haiti. To escape the poverty he and his mother suffered after the death of his father, Dumas moved to Paris for work and discovered theater at the Comédie Française. His resulting career output—writing plays, magazine articles, travel books, essays, and novels—added up to a staggering 100,000 pages. Many of his contemporaries, however, accused the author of running a publishing factory, relying on numerous assistants and collaborators. Be that as it may, Dumas's historic novels *The Count of Monte Cristo* and *The Three Musketeers* were so popular that they were adapted into hundreds of films, translated into many languages, and made the author a fortune during his lifetime. His lavish lifestyle, generous nature, not to mention having over forty mistresses, amassed such a load of debt that Dumas escaped to Belgium, Russia, and Italy between 1851 and 1864. In spite of his personal success, he often faced racist remarks because of his ancestry to which he retorted with wit and humor: "My father was a mulatto, my grandfather was a Negro, and my great-grandfather a monkey. You see, sir, my family starts where yours ends." By the time of his death, Dumas had fallen out of fashion due to changing literary tastes. But on the 200th anniversary of his birth in 2002 French President Jacques Chirac honored the author by having his ashes reinterred at the Panthéon.

Addresses for Dumas

- 25, rue de l'Université (7th)—a white historic plaque is located on the building where Dumas lived on the fifth floor from 1829 to 1831

- Hôtel de Lauzun, then the Hôtel Pimodan, 17, quai d'Anjou (4th)—between 1844 and 1849 Dumas and friends like Baudelaire, Hugo, Balzac, and Delacroix sought expanded consciousness by experimenting with hashish at this mansion

- 20, boulevard des Italiens (9th)—from 1853 to 1857 he had the offices of his newspaper *Le Mousquetaire* upstairs at this address

- Avenue du Président-Kennedy, in Le Port-Marly—address of Dumas's château about an hour's drive west of the city, now a museum

- Place du Général Catroux (17th)—a monument to the author stands at this square

- Le Panthéon, place du Panthéon (5th)—Dumas was re-buried in this place of honor next to authors Hugo and Zola in 2002

Gustave Flaubert (1821-1880)

This writer tirelessly searched for *le mot juste* while avoiding clichés and assonance. In fact, Flaubert's intense dedication to his art prompted essayist Walter Pater to call him a "martyr of style." A doctor's son, Flaubert spent much of his joyless childhood writing in Rouen. Expelled from high school, he nevertheless passed the final exams in 1840 before heading to law school in Paris. Loathing the city and the studies his parents had mapped out for him, he turned his attention to leading a bohemian lifestyle as well as writing and frequenting authors like Victor Hugo. Flaubert's only serious romance was an eight-year relationship with poet Louise Colet. Traveling in Europe, the Middle East, and North Africa, he developed syphilis through contacts with male and female prostitutes. Following an attack of epilepsy in 1846, Flaubert returned home only to lose his father and sister in quick succession. With his new inheritance, however, he was able to devote all of his time to writing. Two friends—authors Maxime Du Camp and Louis Bouilhet—encouraged Flaubert to focus his work on everyday reality. Inspired by a local news item, Flaubert spent five years on his masterpiece *Madame Bovary*, serialized in a Parisian journal in 1856. The government promptly charged the author and publisher with immorality. But thanks to Flaubert's connections in the Second Empire, both were acquitted at trial, boosting the novel's popularity. As the leading exponent of literary realism, Flaubert's influence was great. After his death from a cerebral hemorrhage at age fifty-eight, some of the authors he helped shape—such as Zola, Daudet, and Maupassant—attended his funeral.

Addresses for Flaubert

- Hôtel de l'Europe, once found at 5, rue le Peletier (9th)—in April 1842 Flaubert stayed at this hotel near the Gare Saint Lazare before taking over his friend Ernest Chevalier's apartment at 35, rue de l'Odéon (6th)

- 7, rue de l'Est (20th)—he moved here in the fall of 1842

- Hôtel Sully, 6, rue du Dauphin, now the southern part of the rue Saint-Roch (1st)—former hotel where he stayed whenever accompanied by his mother

- Hôtel Helder, 4, rue Helder (9th)—several times Flaubert rented a room in this hotel, still in operation

- 42, boulevard du Temple (11th)—from 1855 to '69 the author had an expensive apartment at this location

- 18, rue de l'Arcade (8th)—periodically he attended the salon of Madame de Loynes where he first met author George Sand

- 3, rue de la Contrescarpe-Dauphine, now the rue André-Mazet (6th)—Flaubert and Sand—who was the only woman allowed—used to attend dinners with other literary figures at Magny's restaurant formerly at this address

- 4, rue Murillo (8th)—he had an apartment on the fifth floor with a view of Parc Monceau in 1869

- 240, rue du Faubourg Saint-Honoré (8th)—Flaubert had a sixth-floor room without an elevator in 1875

André Gide (1869-1951)

Considered by many as twentieth-century France's greatest man of letters, Gide journeyed from a rigid, puritanical upbringing to becoming a staunch defender of his homosexuality and pedophilia. As the only child of a middle-class Protestant family, the boy studied piano, enjoying summers with relatives in Rouen and Uzès. After the death of his law professor father when Gide was eleven, he had an often strained relationship with his mother. Jotting notes into a diary as a teenager led to prolific writing; by age twenty-one he published his first novel, *The Notebooks of André Walter* (1890). Seven years later a lyrical novel *Les Nourritures terrestres* (*The Fruits of the Earth*) was generally well received. Meanwhile on a personal level, Gide had strong feelings for his cousin Madeleine who became his wife in 1895—although the marriage was never consummated. At around the same time on trips to North Africa he discovered his true physical attraction to young boys which became the subject of a controversial 1902 novel *L'Immoraliste*. In 1917 Gide fell in love with sixteen-year-old Marc Allégret before running away with him to London. In retaliation Gide's wife burned all of his correspondence. A founder and reader for the literary magazine *La Nouvelle Revue Française*, he rejected what he considered the snobbery of Proust's *Swann's Way*, later writing a letter of apology to the author. Like many intellectuals of the time, Gide believed the USSR was the necessary shield to protect against Nazism—until a 1936 visit there changed his mind. André Gide received the Nobel Prize for literature in 1947.

Addresses for Gide

- 19, rue de Médicis, now place Edmond Rostand (6th)—Gide was born at this location near the Luxembourg Gardens

- 2, rue de Tournon (6th)—from 1875 to 1883 he and his family had an apartment on the third floor at this address

- École Alsacienne, 109, rue Notre Dame des Champs (6th)—he started school here before attending the former Pension Keller, 4, rue de Chevreuse (6th) and subsequently the Lycée Henri IV, 23, rue Clovis (5th)

- 4, rue de Commaille (7th)—Gide lived on the fifth floor from 1883 to 1897 before moving to the sixth floor at 4, boulevard Raspail (6th) until 1903 then to #10 on the same street for two years

- 18 bis, avenue des Sycomores (16th)—he moved to the Villa Montmorency in 1906

- 1 bis, rue Vaneau (7th)—Gide lived here from 1926 until his death; a commemorative plaque can be found on the building

Victor Hugo (1801-1885)

Way before *Les Misérables* the musical, there was Victor Hugo's novel in 1862. Thirty years earlier he had written *The Hunchback of Notre*

Dame. But Hugo was even more than a world-class novelist: he was a revered poet, dramatist, artist, and politician. Because of his father's position as a high-ranking officer in Bonaparte's army, the family often left their home in Besançon…until the mother tired of moving and settled with her three sons in Paris. After Victor's first Romantic poems were published at age twenty, he earned a royal pension enabling him to write full time. Ten years later his popular novel on Notre-Dame was in print. Eventually translated into many languages, it would shame officials in the city of Paris into restoring the medieval cathedral. In 1841 Hugo was elected to the Académie Française and, becoming involved in politics, campaigned to abolish the death penalty. After "that villain" Napoléon III's coup d'état in December 1851, the disillusioned author went into exile in Brussels and then moved to the Channel Islands off the coast of Normandy. There in Guernsey he published his most famous work, often referred to nowadays simply as *Les Miz.* On the personal front, Hugo remained married to his wife Adèle for nearly forty-six years, suffered the loss of several children, and engaged in many affairs. His main lover, actress Juliette Drouet, remained a faithful mistress for over five decades. To honor Hugo, one of the most important writers in the French language, nearly two million people lined the streets of the capital at his funeral.

Addresses for Hugo

- 24, rue de Clichy (9th)—in the summer of 1809 Hugo's mother settled here with her children

- 44, rue du Cherche-Midi, at the time 2, rue des Vieilles Tuileries, (6th)—she then moved with her three sons to this address; Hugo returned to live at #39 from 1822 to '24

- 41, rue Sainte-Marguerite, now the rue Trousseau (11th)—in September 1815 he entered school at the Pension Cordier formerly found at this location and later attended the Lycée Louis-le-Grand, 123, rue Saint-Jacques (5th)

- 10, rue des Mézières—Hugo spent the year 1821-1822 here before moving to the fifth floor at 30, rue du Dragon (both in the 6th)

- Le Procope, 13, rue de l'Ancienne-Comédie (6th)—like Balzac, Hugo frequented the oldest café in Paris

- 9, rue Jean-Goujon (8th)—he lived on the third floor of this building with his wife before they moved to 6, place des Vosges, then called place Royale (4th), now a free museum dedicated to the author (see Chapter 3)

- 5, rue de l'Isly (8th)—after their place Royale apartment was ravaged during a workers' uprising, the couple spent a brief time at this address before moving to a spacious apartment at 37 (today # 41), rue de la Tour d'Auvergne (9th) from 1848 to 1851

- 5, avenue Frochot, 66, rue de La Rochefoucauld, (both in the 9th), then to 5, avenue des Sycomores (16th)—addresses where Hugo lived after his return from exile in 1870

- 21, rue de Clichy (9th)—where the author spent the year 1874-1875

- 124, avenue Victor-Hugo, once the avenue d'Eylau (16th)—a white plaque marks this building, which has been replaced, as Hugo's residence from 1878 until his death; the street was renamed for him during his lifetime, a rare honor

- Le Panthéon, place du Panthéon (5th)—Hugo's final resting place in a mausoleum dedicated to the country's greats (also found in Chapter 3)

Stéphane Mallarmé (1842-1898)

The Master of Symbolism, as he was termed, wrote obscure, ambiguous poetry which has been pleasing while confounding readers and translators for over a century. The son of a middle-class family, Mallarmé lost both his mother and his beloved sister at an early age. In 1863, deciding to become an English teacher, he spent nine months in London where he married a German governess. After a series of teaching posts throughout France, in 1871 he settled into a peaceful family life in Paris which was disrupted by the untimely death of his eight-year-old son. During this period friends—including Gide, Valéry, Verlaine, Yeats, and Rilke—started stopping by Mallarmé's home on Tuesdays (*mardis*) to discuss poetry, art and philosophy. Ideas from this salon with the *Mardistes* influenced a generation of writers and musicians. Inspired by the poetry of Hugo and Baudelaire, Mallarmé had been working on the poem "Afternoon of a Faun" for at least ten years before it was finally published. The musicality of the verse so moved Debussy that he created an orchestral masterpiece based on it. In Mallarmé's attempt to decipher the mystery of the world, he abandoned traditional grammar, vocabulary, and syntax, using instead complex metaphors and unconventional typography… especially in his 1897 poem "A Roll of the Dice Will Never Abolish Chance." Toward the end of his life he translated Edgar Allan Poe's "The Raven" into French with illustrations by his friend Manet. Just after receiving the honorific, unofficial title "the prince of poets," Mallarmé died at fifty-six from a spasm of the larynx.

Addresses for Mallarmé

- 12, rue Laferrière (9th)—Étienne Mallarmé was born here

- Pensionnat des Frères des Écoles Chrétiennes, 72, rue Raynouard (16th)—he was a boarding student at this school in Passy between 1852 and 1855

- Collège Rollin, once found at 42, rue des Postes, now the rue Lhomond (5th), Lycée Condorcet, 8, rue du Havre (9th), and Lycée Janson de Sailly, 106, rue de la Pompe (16th)—Mallarmé taught English at these three schools

- 29, rue de Moscou (8th)—beginning in 1871 he and his family lived at this address when he taught at the Lycée Condorcet

- 89, rue de Rome (17th)—from 1875 Mallarmé lived here where he discussed poetry, art, and philosophy with friends at his Tuesday evening salons; a commemorative plaque is on the building.

Guy de Maupassant (1850-1893)

In his short life, "the father of the modern short story" produced a staggering three hundred titles, many of which were eventually adapted to the big screen. Tales with clever plot twists like *The Necklace* inspired future authors such as O. Henry and Henry James. As a schoolboy in Normandy, Maupassant met a family friend Gustave Flaubert who would become his mentor, greatly influencing his writing, especially with the notion of finding *le mot juste*, the right word. In 1869 Maupassant started studying law in Paris, but his education was interrupted by the Franco-Prussian War. During a decade as a clerk at the Ministry of the Navy, he spent nights perfecting his writing. One evening at Flaubert's apartment Maupassant met Émile Zola who invited him to become part of a writers' circle in suburban Médan. The group of six decided to produce a short story collection which would treat events of the war in a realistic way. Maupassant's contribution "Boule de Suif" ("Ball of Tallow") met with immediate, resounding success. For eleven years beginning in 1880 the author became wealthy, producing six novels...as well as several volumes of short stories annually. He frequented other writers like Mallarmé, Proust, and the son of Alexandre Dumas, but never gave up on his pastimes: hunting, traveling, boating, and chasing women. By 1891, however, possibly from a combination of syphilis and the use of hallucinogenic drugs, his mental health began to suffer. After an 1892 suicide attempt, Maupassant was confined to a private psychiatric hospital where he died one month before his forty-third birthday.

Addresses for Maupassant

- 2, rue de Moncey (9th)—from 1872 to 1876 Maupassant lived in a tiny, dark room on the ground floor at this address

- 17, rue Clauzel (9th)—beginning in 1876 he had a third-floor apartment where he read "Boule de Suif" to his literary friends; due to an error, a memorial plaque was for a long time affixed at #19

- 83, rue Dulong and 10, rue Montchanin, now rue Jacques Bingen (both in the 17th)—two apartments where the author resided

- 14, avenue Victor Hugo (16th)—Maupassant lived here for a short while from 1889 to 1890 but because of the noise from a downstairs bakery, he soon moved to the third floor at 24, rue du Boccador (8th)

- Ministère de la Marine, 2, rue Royale (8th)—he spent ten years working in the Navy department as a clerk and later with the help of Flaubert got a job at the Ministère de l'Instruction publique [now de l'Éducation nationale] at 110, rue de Grenelle (7th)

- 17, rue Berton (16th)—Maupassant's mother arranged to have him examined by Dr. Charcot at his clinic in 1892

- 16, avenue de Lamballe (16th)—he lived at a private psychiatric hospital at this address until his death; a historic plaque marks the building

- Église Saint-Pierre-de-Chaillot, 31, avenue Marceau (16th)—Maupassant's funeral was held at this church; Zola delivered the eulogy

- Cimetière du Montparnasse, 3, boulevard Edgar Quinet (14th)—the author is buried in division 26 of this cemetery

- Parc Monceau, 35, boulevard de Courcelles (8th)—a monument to Maupassant can be found in this park, a short walk from the Arc de Triomphe

Jacques Prévert (1900-1977)

Before Bing Crosby, Doris Day, and Nat King Cole recorded the popular tune "Autumn Leaves," there was the poem "Les Feuilles mortes" by Prévert. Set to music by his friend Joseph Kosma, the song was later translated into English by Johnny Mercer. A middle-class child, Prévert was bored at school, often skipping class before dropping out definitively at age fifteen. At Adrienne Monnier's bookshop in the early 1920s he met some Surrealist poets who would greatly influence his poetry. From 1924 to 1928 Prévert lived at an army buddy's house on the rue du Château in the 14th where a group of like-minded painters and poets exchanged ideas. There, they also played his collective writing and drawing game called the "cadaver exquis" ("exquisite cadaver"). After getting married in 1928, Prévert moved with his wife to Montmartre and started writing. When an actor friend needed a screenplay, he took the job, launching a career as an innovative scriptwriter on films such as *Les Enfants du Paradis* for which he received an Oscar nomination. In 1946 an editor convinced Prévert to combine the poems he had published in various journals into a collection called *Paroles*. The success was immediate and overwhelming...with 5,000 copies sold in a matter of weeks. Translated into many languages, the themes of simple joys, love, and revolt expressed through creative word play and humor resonated internationally. An accidental fall out of a window in 1948 initiated Prévert's third career: making collages which were exhibited at several Parisian galleries. A three-pack-a-day smoker, he died of lung cancer at age seventy-seven.

Addresses for Prévert

- 19, rue de Chartres, Neuilly-sur-Seine—Prévert was born just outside the city limits of Paris near the Bois de Boulogne

- 7, rue de Vaugirard—the family found top-floor living quarters here in 1907 before moving the next year to 4, rue Férou and then in 1912 to 5, rue Tournon and 7, rue du Vieux-Colombier (all in the 6th)

- Jardins du Luxembourg, 15, rue de Vaugirard (6th)—his favorite park near the family home

- Église Saint-Sulpice, 2, rue Palatine (6th)—the family's neighborhood church

- Odéon Théâtre de l'Europe, formerly Théâtre national de l'Odéon, 1, place de l'Odéon—his father used to bring him to see plays at this theater, giving him an interest in the arts and influencing his future writing, and to the café Les Deux Magots,

6, place Saint-Germain-des-Prés (both in the 6th)

- Le Bon Marché, 38, rue de Sèvres (7th)—after dropping out of school, he "moved objects" at this department store before getting fired for tardiness and bad behavior

- Maison des Amis des Livres, formerly at 7, rue de l'Odéon (6th)— beginning in 1923 he frequented Adrienne Monnier's bookshop where he met Surrealist poets André Breton and Louis Aragon

- 54, rue du Château (14th)—in the 1920s a Symbolist and Surrealist group of painters and poets lived in actor Marcel Duhamel's house where they played Prévert's "cadavre exquis"

- 47, avenue Junot (18th)—Prévert and his wife had a tiny apartment in Montmartre before actor Pierre Batcheff invited them to live at his house on the square de Robiac (7th)

- 39, rue Dauphine (6th)—from 1931 to '32 the couple had a place on fifth floor at this address

- 6 bis, Cité Véron (18th)—after living in hotels, Prévert settled at this location in 1956

- Galerie Maeght, 42, rue du Bac (7th)—in 1957 there was an exhibition of Prévert's collages at this gallery; a similar show followed in 1963 at the former Galerie Knoedler at 85 bis, rue du Faubourg-Saint-Honoré (8th)

Marcel Proust (1871-1922)

Author Anatole France supposedly declared: "Life is short; Proust is long." Even if the quote is fictitious, it certainly has a ring of truth about it. For Proust's masterpiece *In Search of Lost Time* clocks in at an astounding seven volumes, 3,000 pages, and 2,000 characters. Growing up in a well-to-do family, Proust suffered from serious respiratory problems. Yet he published in journals as a schoolboy and founded the review *Le Banquet* in 1892. The young Proust frequented writers and artists at salons and gained a reputation as a dilettante, snob, and social climber. His first novel, at age twenty-four, went unpublished until after his death. Proust's admiration for John Ruskin led to translating two of the British art critic's works into French. The death of his beloved mother in 1905 left Proust with a considerable inheritance allowing him to begin writing his monumental work. We can imagine the author sitting in his cork-lined bedroom (which soundproofed the space and kept out allergens which triggered his asthma), reliving memories of childhood days at his father's birthplace at Illiers—including the famous recollection about the Madeleine sponge cake. Volume one, *Swann's Way*, was not accepted by Gallimard for publication mainly due to André Gide's panning of the work, for which he later apologized. Proust shared his love of music, art, and literature with Venezuelan composer Reynaldo Hahn during their two-year romantic relationship. One of the most influential writers of the twentieth century, Proust received the Prix Goncourt three years before his death from pneumonia and bronchitis at age fifty-one.

Addresses for Proust

- 96, rue La Fontaine, now avenue Mozart (16th)—Proust was born in his great-uncle's house at this location in Auteuil

- 9, boulevard Malesherbes (8th)—from 1873 to 1900 he lived with his family in a Haussmannian building

- Lycée Condorcet, 8, rue du Havre (9th)—although sickly, he excelled at this high school near the Gare Saint-Lazare

- Bibliothèque Mazarine, 23, quai de Conti (6th)—Proust's father got his son a volunteer position at this library in 1896 though he never actually went to work there

- 31, rue de Monceau (8th)—he attended the salon of Madeleine Lemaire at this address

- 45, rue de Courcelles (8th)—when Proust was twenty-nine, he and his mother moved here

- 102, boulevard Haussmann (8th)—from 1907 to 1919 he lived in a room lined with cork from walls to ceiling at this address; a memorial plaque is located on the building

- 8 bis, rue Laurent-Pichat (16th)—for three months in 1919 he rented an apartment from his friend actress Réjane

- Pavillon d'Armenonville, allée de Longchamp (16th)—this location in the Bois de Boulogne once housed a restaurant Proust frequented

- 44, rue de l'Amiral Hamelin (16th)—where the author spent the last three years of his life, sleeping during the day and writing at night

- Musée Carnavalet, 16, rue des Francs-Bourgeois (3rd)—some of Proust's furnishings can be found at this free museum dedicated to the history of Paris

- Cimetière du Père Lachaise, 16, rue du Repos (20th)—Proust is buried alongside his family in division 85 of this cemetery

Arthur Rimbaud (1854-1891)

This precocious "enfant terrible" was just a teenager when he began astonishing the Parisian literary scene with his poetry as well as scandalizing them with his rude behavior. His childhood in a town north of Reims was marked by a father who abandoned the family and a rigid, controlling mother. An excellent student encouraged to write verses by a tutor, Rimbaud published his first poem at fifteen. The following year he ran away to Paris for the first of three times. Taking the train without a ticket landed him in jail before his tutor arranged for his release ten days later. The sixteen-year-old Rimbaud also composed the symbolist gem "Le Bateau Ivre" ("The Drunken Boat"), inspired by the works of Jules Verne. His synesthetic "Voyelles"—from the same period—attributed a color to each vowel of the alphabet. At a friend's suggestion in September '71 Rimbaud sent a letter and a few poems to Paul Verlaine who mailed him a one-way ticket to the capital. The handsome, blue-eyed Rimbaud soon became the lover of Verlaine, ten years his senior. During their two-year relationship the couple lived a wild, vagabond life, fueled by absinthe, hashish, and opium; at least one writer described the duo as "pimps and thieves."

At the end of their stormy liaison a jealous, inebriated Verlaine shot his young lover in the wrist at a Brussels hotel —a crime for which he spent eighteen months in jail. When Rimbaud was twenty, he gave up poetry for good, preferring a life of reading, travel, and language study. He died of bone cancer at age thirty-seven.

Addresses for Rimbaud

- Prison Mazas, 23-25, boulevard Mazas, now the boulevard Diderot (12th)—after taking the train without a ticket, Rimbaud was confined to a prison once found near the Gare de Lyon
- 14, rue Nicolet (18th)—he stayed for three weeks with Verlaine and his wife at the home of Verlaine's in-laws before being asked to leave
- 72 bis, rue Bonaparte (6th)—site of Rimbaud's first reading of his poem "Le Bateau Ivre" in 1871; a plaque notes the event
- Hôtel des Étrangers, now the Belloy Saint-Germain, 2, rue Racine (6th)—the Zutistes, a circle of poets which included Verlaine and Rimbaud, met at this address
- Hôtel de Cluny, now the Cluny Sorbonne, 8, rue Victor Cousin (5th)—a plaque states that in June 1872 Rimbaud wrote "at this time I have a pretty room" at this hotel
- 4, rue Férou (6th)—a wall poem of "Le Bateau Ivre" is located here

Antoine de Saint-Exupéry (1900-1944)

"Saint-Ex" was doubly gifted—as an author and an aviator. But life wasn't always easy. His father's death before the boy was four forced the family to live as impoverished aristocrats. Although creative, he didn't excel in school. Twice he failed exams to enter the École Navale and audited courses at the École des Beaux-Arts without getting a degree. Things turned around for Saint-Exupéry during military service when he learned to fly. A pioneer pilot for Aéropostale, he delivered mail throughout Europe, Africa, and South America. This real-life hero often had the unenviable task of rescuing downed pilots in remote locations. All the while he wrote, centering much of his work on personal experiences. *Night Flight*, an international best seller about the bravery of pilots, confirmed his status as a rising literary star. In New York after France's armistice with Germany, Saint-Exupéry composed and illustrated his most famous piece: *The Little Prince* (1942). The novella, based in part on his actual crash landing in the Libyan dessert, is one of the best-selling books of all time. Many critics believe the story's vain, ill-tempered Rose reflects the turbulent relationship between Saint-Ex and his wife. The same year *The Little Prince* was published, the author penned an "Open Letter to Frenchmen Everywhere" asking for unity against Nazi oppression. With his mental and physical health deteriorating, in 1944 he flew reconnaissance missions in France. On July 31 of that year Saint-Exupéry's plane went down and its fragments were only recently discovered. He lived according to his words: "To be a man is, precisely, to be responsible."

Addresses for Saint-Exupéry

- Lycée Saint-Louis, 44, boulevard Saint-Michel (6th)—Saint-Ex attended this school to prepare for entrance to the École Navale

- 10, rue de Castellane (8th)—he and his wife Consuelo lived here from 1931 to '34

- 5, rue Chanaleilles and Hôtel Pont-Royal, 5-7, rue de Montal-embert (both in the 7th)—two other locations associated with the author

- 15, place Vauban (7th)—from 1934 to 1940 Saint-Ex lived at this address where visitors can find a memorial plaque

- Deux Magots, 6, place Saint-Germain-des-Prés, Brasserie Lipp, 151, boulevard Saint-Germain (both in the 6th), and La Coupole, 102, boulevard du Montparnasse (14th)—favorite cafés of the couple

- 52, rue de Michel-Ange (16th)—during one of the many splits from his wife, Saint-Exupéry lived here alone

- 1, avenue de la Motte Picquet, square Santiago du Chili (7th)—a bust of the author is located at this address

- Musée de l'Air et de l'Espace, in the airport at Le Bourget, a half-hour drive from the center of Paris—articles found in the wreckage of his plane were donated to this air and space museum along with other artifacts commemorating his life

- Le Panthéon, place du Panthéon (5th)—since Saint-Exupéry's body was never officially recovered, a simple plaque is dedicated to him at this mausoleum honoring France's distinguished citizens (read more about the Panthéon in Chapter 3)

George Sand [Aurore Dupin] (1804-1876)

No other contemporaries could boast about their works being more popular than Balzac's...nor about their first novel outselling Victor Hugo's *The Hunchback of Notre Dame*. No one but Aurore Dupin, that is, under the pseudonym George Sand. But early years would have suggested otherwise. Raised mainly by her grandmother in Nohant (three hours south of Paris), at eighteen she committed to an unhappy marriage soon giving birth to two children. Separated from her abusive husband, she and writer Jules Sandeau became lovers and collaborated on a novel using the name "J. Sand." The book enjoyed enough popularity to prompt a second editor to ask for more. The twenty-seven-year-old Dupin struck a compromise: to publish her novel *Indiana* using the same surname but changing the first name to indicate a different author. The feminist work was immediately successful, drawing praise from Dumas and Balzac. Sand shocked nineteenth-century society with the subversive tone of her writing... in addition to wearing men's clothes, smoking cigars and cigarettes in public, and having a great number of affairs. Two of her liaisons involved authors Prosper Mérimée and Alfred de Musset. The eight years she spent with Frédéric Chopin formed the basis for her travel novel *A Winter in Majorca*. By producing over seventy novels, as well as autobiographical works, literary criticism, and political texts, Sand became the most prolific female writer in the history of literature— respected internationally by Dostoevsky, Elizabeth Barrett Browning, and Walt Whitman. Giving the eulogy at her funeral, Victor Hugo proclaimed her a poet: "the lyre was within her." However, the discussion of moving Sand's remains to the Panthéon has twice met with opposition from the citizens of Nohant.

Addresses for Sand

- 46, rue Meslay, at the time #15 (3rd)—a plaque marks the birthplace of Aurore Dupin

- 13, rue de la Grange-Batelière (9th)—she spent her first three years in a small home at this address which she recounts in her autobiography *Histoire de ma vie*

- Le Couvent des Dames Augustines Anglaises, rue Fossés-Saint-Victor, now 55-63, rue du Cardinal-Lemoine (5th)—her grandmother sent the rebellious thirteen-year-old Aurore to school at this convent for two years

- Théâtre des Variétés, 7, boulevard Montmartre (2nd)—her mother often brought her to shows at this theater, still in operation

- Hôtel George Sand, 26, formerly #56, rue des Mathurins (9th)—then called the Hôtel Florence, Sand gave birth to her son here

- 21, quai des Grands Augustins (6th)—she shared this location with Jules Sandeau in 1830 before moving to the sixth floor at 29 (then #25), quai Saint-Michel (5th)

- 31, rue de Seine (6th)—a commemorative plaque indicates that the author lived here in 1831

- Restaurant Lointier, once found at 104, rue de Richelieu (2nd)—she first met Alfred de Musset at this restaurant in June 1833

- 19, quai Malaquais (6th)—from 1832 to 1836 Sand lived at this address, some of the time with Musset

- Hôtel de France, 21-23, rue Lafitte (9th)—in October 1836 she moved to this former hotel

- 16, rue Jean-Baptiste-Pigalle (9th)—Sand and Chopin lived at this address from 1839 to 1842

- 5, square d'Orléans, (9th)—a memorial plaque indicates she lived on the second floor from 1842 to 1847, before moving to 8, rue de Condé (6th) in 1848

- 3, rue Racine (6th)—between 1851 to 1864 she had apartments on the third followed by the fifth floor then moved to 90, rue Claude-Bernard (5th)

- 5, rue Gay-Lussac (5th)—she lived at this address from 1865 to 1871

- 18, rue de l'Arcade (8th)—Sand first met Gustave Flaubert at the salon of Madame de Loynes

- 3, rue de la Contrescarpe-Dauphine, now the rue André-Mazet (6th)—Flaubert and Sand—who was the only woman allowed—used to attend dinners with other literary figures at Magny's restaurant formerly at this address

Jean-Paul Sartre (1905-1980)

Here's one philosopher who is equally well-known in the literary world. Born into a bourgeois family, the young boy experienced the death of his father and lost most of his vision in one eye due to illness. As a result, "Poulou," as he was called, was coddled by his mother and grandparents. Sartre's early studies came from his grandfather's immense library. When the ten-year-old boy arrived at public school, he was a diligent worker. However, Sartre surprised graduate school friends (and no doubt himself) by failing his *agrégation* final exam in 1928. While preparing for a second try, he was in a study group with Simone de Beauvoir, launching a fifty-year non-monogamous relationship. *Le Mur*, a book of short studies published in 1939, was termed a masterpiece by André Gide. That same year Sartre was mobilized and became a prisoner of war, where the sense of community he discovered with fellow soldiers would form part of his existentialist philosophy. He found fame in the '40s with the publication of the play *No Exit*. After the war Sartre became politically active and, until the Soviet invasion of Budapest, wrote in favor of communism. In 1964 he became the first person to refuse the Nobel Prize for literature stating: "no man deserves to be consecrated during his lifetime." Physically depleted from overwork, alcohol, tobacco, and drug abuse, Sartre suffered two strokes in the early '70s and was left virtually blind. His legacy includes novels, essays, plays, philosophical and biographical texts, plus his founding the journal *Les Temps modernes* and the newspaper *Libération*.

Addresses for Sartre

- 13, rue Mignard (16th)—Sartre was born at his grandparents' house at this address

- 1, rue Le Goff (5th)—he lived with his family on the seventh floor of this building

- Lycée Montaigne, 17, rue Auguste Comte (6th)—he briefly attended this high school before transferring to Lycée Henri IV, 23, rue Clovis (5th) at age sixteen

- Lycée Louis le Grand, 123, rue Saint-Jacques (5th)—at this school he prepared for entrance into the École normale supérieure, 45, rue d'Ulm (5th), a very selective graduate school to prepare teachers

- 23, avenue de Lamballe (16th)—after his release as a prisoner of war, he stayed at his mother's apartment here

- Café de Flore, 172, boulevard Saint-Germain-des-Prés (6th)—a favorite hangout for Sartre and Beauvoir

- Hôtel Mistral, 24, rue de Cels (14th)—a plaque at this hotel indicates that the couple lived here on several occasions

- Lycée Condorcet, 8, rue du Havre (9th)—he taught here in 1941

- Hôtel La Louisiane, 60, rue de Seine (6th)—Sartre and Beauvoir had separate rooms at this hotel in 1943

- Théâtre du Vieux-Colombier, 21, rue du Vieux-Colombier (6th)—his play *Huis Clos* (*No Exit*) was first performed here on May 27, 1944

- 42, rue Bonaparte (6th)—he and his mother lived on the fifth floor of this building from 1945 to 1962

- 222, boulevard Raspail (14th)—after right-wing attacks on his building on the rue Bonaparte, he moved to a hotel once found here in 1962

- 29, boulevard Edgar-Quinet (14th)—in 1969 Sartre lived on the eleventh floor at this address

- Cimetière du Montparnasse, 3, boulevard Edgar Quinet (14th)— 50,000 people lined the streets of Paris the day of his burial in the 20th division of this cemetery

Paul Verlaine (1844-1896)

In his essay about "accursed poets" (*Les Poètes maudits*), Verlaine described writers living a life which differed from societal norms. Including himself under the anagrammed name "Pauvre Lélian," he fit right in because of his addictions to drugs and alcohol as well as a propensity toward violence. An only child in Metz, he was raised alongside his beloved cousin Élisa. Once the family settled in Paris, Verlaine wrote his first poem at fourteen. He attended law classes but clearly preferred the literary circles found in cafés. In 1866 under the influence of Baudelaire the young man published twenty-five *Poèmes saturniens* which established him as an up-and-coming poet. A famous poem from that collection "Chanson d'automne" ("Song of Autumn") was used by the British seventy-eight years later to signal D-Day to the French Resistance. The death of Élisa in childbirth threw Verlaine into the severe alcoholism which would plague him for the rest of his life. In 1870 he married and became a father, but abandoned his family the following year after meeting a young admirer of his poetry, Arthur Rimbaud. During their tempestuous two-year relationship, the men moved to London and then to Brussels where in a drunken, jealous rage Verlaine shot his lover in the wrist. After eighteen months in a Belgian jail, Verlaine took teaching jobs in England where he developed a deep affection for one of his students. The poet's final years, even though tormented by drugs, alcohol, and poverty, were also crowned with success. His peers gave him the honorific title "prince of poets" and his work inspired several musical compositions including Debussy's "Clair de lune." Verlaine died of pneumonia at age fifty-one.

Addresses for Verlaine

- 10, rue des Petites-Écuries (10th)—the boy and his family first lived here after moving from Metz

- Institution Landry, formerly found at 32, rue Chaptal (9th)— he was a boarding student at this school for nine years before attending the Lycée Condorcet, 8, rue du Havre (9th) then called Lycée Bonaparte

- 10, rue Nollet, formerly the rue Saint-Louis (17th)—as an adolescent he lived with his family at this address before moving to 45, rue Lemercier (17th)

- 10, boulevard des Batignolles (17th)—he frequented the literary salon of Madame de Ricard, the mother of a friend

- 14, rue Lécluse (17th)—the family lived here until the death of his father when Verlaine and his mother moved to #26 on the same street

- 14, rue Nicolet (18th)—Verlaine and his wife lived here (for three weeks with Rimbaud) with her parents

- Café François 1er, 69, boulevard Saint-Michel (5th)—Verlaine was once photographed at this former café

- 39, rue Descartes (5th)—a memorial plaque indicates where the poet lived and died

- Église Saint-Étienne-du-Mont, 6, place Sainte-Geneviève (5th)— his funeral was held at this church in 1896

- Cimetière des Batignolles, 8, rue Saint-Just (17th)—Verlaine is buried in the 11th division of this cemetery

Jules Verne (1828-1905)

Twenty Thousand Leagues Under the Sea and *Journey to the Center of the Earth* are just two of the well-known works by this prolific author. An excellent student at religious schools in Nantes, Verne enjoyed reading Daniel Defoe's *Robinson Crusoe*, the plays of Victor Hugo, as well as the novels of James Fenimore Cooper. The teen showed an early interest in writing but was persuaded to pursue the family business by studying law in Paris. Introduced to the capital's literary salons, he found a father-figure and mentor in author Alexandre Dumas. After receiving his law degree in 1851, Verne discovered that the editor of *Musée des Familles* magazine needed someone to write stories based on geography, history, science, and technology. He had finally found his niche. Throwing himself into research at the Bibliothèque Nationale, Verne began a lifelong habit of jotting down scientific and historic facts on notecards. Around this time he met explorer Jacques Arago whose witty travel tales inspired Verne to develop the geographic adventure novel. In 1863 publisher Pierre-Jules Hetzel serialized Verne's *Five Weeks in a Balloon* in his magazine before bringing it out in book form, a practice which would continue with all of the author's subsequent works. Adapting novels like *Around the World in Eighty Days* for the stage proved most lucrative for Verne. Wealthy and famous in his lifetime, he was able to sail around Europe in a series of boats all of which he named "Saint-Michel." Besides being a pioneer in the field of science fiction, Verne had a profound influence on the Surrealist movement.

Addresses for Verne

- 2, rue Thérèse (1ˢᵗ)—while studying law in 1847, he stayed with his great-aunt here
- 24, rue de l'Ancienne-Comédie, the number no longer exists (6ᵗʰ)— in 1848 Verne rented an apartment with another student from Nantes on the fourth floor at this address before moving to the seventh floor at 18, boulevard de la Bonne-Nouvelle (10ᵗʰ)

- Théâtre Lyrique, 72, boulevard du Temple, now 10, place de la République (11th)—Dumas helped him get a job as a secretary to the director at this theater where Verne also put on his own plays

- Bibliothèque Nationale, 58, rue de Richelieu (2nd)—Verne researched works for the magazine *Musée des Familles* at the national library

- 72, rue de Provence (9th)—to earn extra money he worked for broker Fernand Eggly in 1856

- 18, boulevard Poissonnière (9th)—Verne and his wife Honorine settled here for a few months in 1857 before moving to rue Saint-Martin then to 54, rue du Faubourg Montmartre (9th), 45, boulevard de Magenta (10th), and 18, passage (now rue) Saulnier (9th)

- 18, rue Jacob (6th)—in the fall of 1862 he visited the office of Pierre-Jules Hetzel who published *Five Weeks in a Balloon*

- 39, rue La Fontaine (16th)—Verne lived here from 1863 to '69

- Théâtre de la Porte Saint Martin, 18, boulevard Saint-Martin (10th)—still in operation, this theater was the site of the staged version of *Around the World in Eighty Days* which played to packed houses

- Hôtel du Louvre, place André Malraux (1st)—Verne preferred to stay at this hotel later in life when he came to Paris from his home in Amiens

Émile Zola (1840-1902)

Nulla dies sine linea ("not a day without a line") was Zola's motto. And writing at least one line every day helped him accomplish his ambitious series describing five generations of the Rougon-Macquart family. Son of an Italian engineer, he spent his first three years in Paris before the family moved south to Aix-en-Provence. Left practically penniless after his father's death, he and his mother found their way back to the capital. Zola twice failed final high school exams, but continued his education by reading great writers. The teenager felt isolated in Paris until friends from Aix, including the artist Cézanne, came to town. Of all Zola's early jobs the four years at Hachette publishers were the most fruitful for his career. Not only did he make valuable literary contacts, but he also learned the importance of publicizing one's work. During this time he honed his skills writing reviews and articles on literature, art, and politics. Once the twenty-eight-year-old Zola published his novel *Thérèse Raquin*, he laid out plans to produce twenty works documenting the seamy side of life under the Second Empire. As the leader of French Naturalism he drew from science—using meticulous observation to portray his multiple characters. In January 1898 Zola risked his career (and possibly his life) by writing "J'accuse," a letter in a Parisian newspaper blaming the French army for obstructing justice in the case of Captain Alfred Dreyfus. Zola's death from carbon monoxide poisoning because of a blocked chimney was either an accident or an act of retribution because of his involvement in the Dreyfus Affair.

Addresses for Zola

- 10, rue Saint-Joseph (2nd)—Zola was born and lived the first three years of his life on the fifth floor of this building; a commemorative plaque is here

- Lycée Saint-Louis, 44, boulevard Saint-Michel (6th)—he attended this high school but failed the *bac* exams twice

- 63, rue Monsieur-le-Prince (6th)—from 1858 to '59 the Zola family lived here before moving to 241, rue Saint-Jacques in 1859 and then to 35, rue Saint-Victor (both in the 5th)

- 7, rue des Feuillantines (5th)—in 1863 Zola, who shared this apartment with his mother, started having Thursday evening gatherings with friends like Paul Cézanne; he would continue similar meetings with writers after moving to suburban Médan in 1880

- Café Guerbois, 9, avenue de Clichy, once the grande rue des Batignolles (18th)—he often joined his Impressionist friends, then called the Groupe des Baignolles, at this café

- 14, rue la Condamine (17th)—Zola lived in a small house once found here several times between 1869 and 1871

- 10, rue de Vaugirard (6th)—he and his wife Gabrielle first lived at this address

- 144, rue Montmartre (2nd)—a plaque marks the offices of *Aurore* newspaper where Zola brought a copy of his letter *J'accuse*

- 21 bis, rue de Bruxelles (9th)—he lived here from 1889 until his death from carbon monoxide poisoning because of a blocked chimney in the bedroom; another plaque is found at this location

- Cimetière de Montmartre, 20, avenue Rachel (18th)—Zola's tomb is located in this cemetery but on June 4, 1908 his remains were transferred to the Panthéon, place du Panthéon (5th) where he shares a crypt with Hugo and Dumas

Chapter 8

Chefs and Food Critics

WHILE REFLECTING ON THE fourteen years he spent in the French capital, Art Buchwald once remarked: "whoever goes there takes away the greatest meal he has ever had in his life." Not to contradict the famed journalist, but as is true in any big city, great and not-so-great offerings are plentiful in Paris. This chapter intends to look at some of the most renowned figures in the history of great Parisian cuisine. Many earning superlative titles like "the Prince of Gastronomy," "the King of Chefs," or "the Chef of the Century," all six individuals found in these pages did their part in creating the top restaurants and bakeries…or in Curnonsky's case in helping direct gourmets to their location. Among other big names included in this chapter you'll find Escoffier, Pépin, and Robuchon. So have some fun at least dreaming about the kind of meal you'd order if you were ever fortunate enough to visit establishments such as these. Et bon appétit!

Curnonsky [Maurice Edmond Sailland] (1872-1956)

When over 3,000 chefs and other connoisseurs name you "the Prince of Gastronomy," well, that's saying something. In 1927 that very title was awarded to Curnonsky. The esteemed food writer learned early on from the family maid to examine products closely and cook them to perfection. Originally going to Paris to study literature at the Sorbonne, he was talked into journalism by friends. He then served as a ghostwriter on many projects, including work with Willy, one-time husband of author Colette. Later, he combined his journalistic skills with his love of food, choosing the pseudonym Curnonsky—a combination of Latin and French words for "why not," adding "sky" at the end to mimic the vogue for Russian at the time. Curnonsky's tall, corpulent physique was matched by his considerable literary output: novels, short stories, and magazine articles. Not to mention the twenty-eight-volume *France Gastronomique* he co-wrote with a friend after they spent nine years evaluating regional restaurants throughout the country. The author also traveled abroad, introducing the idea of culinary tourism from trips to places like China whose cuisine he considered the best in the world. In later life he had a boiled egg for breakfast and a full meal in a Parisian restaurant at night where owners were undoubtedly avid for his commendations. Although Julia Child found Curnonsky "a big bag of wind," I think he was right on target with his preference for simple, country fare saying: "you can keep those elaborate dinners that pass for *grande cuisine*." The Légion d'honneur recipient died falling out of his apartment window at age eighty-four.

Addresses for Curnonsky

- 129, rue du Faubourg Saint-Honoré (8th)—the Cordon Bleu first opened for classes at this location where Curnonsky studied with chef Henri-Paul Pellaprat

- 14, place Henri Bergson (8th)—address where the food writer lived and died, marked with a commemorative plaque

- Chez Pierre, 10, rue Richelieu and Chez Pauline, 50, rue Villédo (both in the 1st)—he enjoyed meals at these restaurants which have naturally changed hands since that time

- Maxim's, 3, rue Royale (8th) and La Closerie des Lilas, 171, boulevard du Montparnasse (6th)—two "institutions" in the Parisian dining world which Curnonsky sometimes visited

Auguste Escoffier (1846-1935)

The "King of Chefs" holds that title for many reasons. For one, his 1903 *Guide Culinaire* is still used worldwide in many culinary schools. As a boy, though, he was interested in art...later evident in his hobby of making wax flowers. At thirteen he was sent to apprentice in his uncle's kitchen in Nice. Escoffier vowed, that when in charge, he would improve working conditions for staff by eliminating shouting and the drinking of alcohol on the job. In another restaurant nearby, he was discovered by the Parisian owner of Le Petit Moulin Rouge who hired the teenager as an apprentice. Escoffier worked in Paris for over a year before being drafted into the army; there, the importance of preserving food led to his creation of canned tomatoes. Back at the Moulin, he spent five years as chef de cuisine where he befriended actress Sarah Bernhardt. Once he left the French capital for Monte Carlo in 1884, Escoffier began a partnership with Swiss hotelier César Ritz. The inseparable friends developed international luxury hospitality in various places. London's Savoy Hotel, for instance, attracted aristocrats and celebrities like Australian soprano Nellie Melba, for whom Escoffier created his Pêche Melba dessert. After getting fired for defrauding the Savoy of wine and food, the partners inaugurated the French capital's Hôtel Ritz. Lavishness, service, and fine dining resulted in "ritzy" being added to the English language. Escoffier is remembered for his recipes using seasonal ingredients, the prix fixe menu, the organization of professional kitchens, and elevating the profession in the eyes of the public.

Addresses for Escoffier

- Le Petit Moulin Rouge, formerly found at 17, rue d'Antin (2nd)—restaurant where Escoffier first apprenticed in Paris (no relation to the cabaret in Montmartre)

- Le Skating, 15, rue Blanche (9th)—former roller-skating rink/theater where he displayed some of his exquisite wax flowers at a culinary exhibition in December 1882

- rue Boissy d'Anglas (8th)—Escoffier had an apartment on this street (no number found)

- Hôtel Ritz, 15, place Vendôme (1st)—Ritz and Escoffier opened this hotel/restaurant for business in June 1898 (read more about it in Chapters 1 and 2)

Michel Guérard (1933-)

French chef turned health food guru? Yes, and what a trajectory it was. As a boy outside Rouen, he delighted in his grandmother's cooking. So, in 1947 he took an apprenticeship at a pastry shop northwest of the capital. At age twenty-five he became the head dessert chef at Paris's luxurious Hôtel Crillon; just two years later he was named the best pastry chef in France. Guérard had positions at some of the finest kitchens in Paris before opening his suburban restaurant Le Pot-au-Feu in 1965. After the rationing years of WWII, menu items had become loaded with butter and cream. By the late '60s, however, some chefs like Guérard began proposing lighter fare termed *Nouvelle Cuisine*. His offerings caught on big time and his restaurant was awarded one Michelin star in '67 and a second in '71. Another change of course came in 1974 after his marriage and move south to the spa village of Eugénie-les-Bains. There, to please dieting and health-conscious patrons, Guérard created his *Grande Cuisine Minceur*...or "gastronomy for weight-watchers." The outrage at altering French classics was immediate; he was regarded, he says, as "at worst an outcast and at best a crazy cook." By 1976 however, Guérard appeared on the cover of the European edition of *Time* magazine. One year later his main restaurant had won three Michelin stars which, incredibly, it has maintained ever since. In 2013 he opened the Michel Guérard Institute, a school devoted to preparing healthy meals. An energetic man, he extols the importance of passion for your work: "You can continue for a long time as long as you are not bored."

Addresses for Guérard

- Hôtel Crillon, 10, place de la Concorde (8th)—in 1957 Guérard became head pastry chef at this hotel's restaurant

- Maxim's, 3, rue Royale (8th)—he worked at this famous location along with positions at other restaurants such as the Lucas Carton, 9, place de la Madeleine (8th). Lapérouse, 51, quai des Grands Augustins (6th), and the cabaret Le Lido, 116, avenue des Champs-Élysées (8th)

Jacques Pépin (1935-)

A celebrity chef in the United States, Pépin is well known for his cookbooks, television shows, and collaborations with Julia Child. But before finding fame stateside, he had a sparkling résumé in his home country. In his native Bourg-en-Bresse (not far from Mâcon), the young boy learned to have "respect for ingredients" while helping out in his mother's restaurant at Hôtel L'Amour. The family soon moved to Lyon where he continued to work part-time in the kitchen—at Chez Pépin in 1947 and later at Le Pélican. Deciding to become a chef when he was thirteen, Pépin trained at the Grand Hôtel de l'Europe in his hometown. An apprentice's job, he tells us, is far from glamorous: "you clean, you scale fish, you kill and pluck chicken." Through observation and practice, though, after one year the teenager was promoted to the stove. Pépin then moved to Paris, training at some of the capital's most renowned restaurants—from the Plaza Athénée to Maxim's and Le Fouquet's. Because of his membership in an organization called La Société des cuisiniers, he got a variety of experiences filling in where needed from the Salvation Army's soup kitchen to the restaurant of Galeries Lafayette department store. From 1956 to 1958 Pépin became the personal chef to several French prime ministers, including Charles de Gaulle (see Chapter 12). During this period, heads of state, such as Eisenhower, Nehru, Tito, and Macmillan, dined on Pépin's cuisine. But he says chefs of the time, being "at the bottom of the social scale," were never invited out of the kitchen.

Addresses for Pépin

- 48, rue Pierre Charron (8th)—site of Pépin's small room in Paris
- La Société des Cuisiniers, 28, rue de la Sourdière (1st)—former

address of the association which continues to find temporary employment for chefs

- Le Meurice, 228, rue de Rivoli (1st)—Pépin had his first exposure to haute cuisine at this restaurant, currently run by chef Alain Ducasse

- Hôtel Plaza Athénée, 25, avenue Montaigne (8th)—at seventeen he trained at the restaurant of this luxury hotel under Lucien Diat, who demanded flawless precision; also now headed by Ducasse

- Maxim's, 3, rue Royale (8th) and Le Fouquet's, 99, avenue des Champs-Élysées (8th)—two world-famous restaurants where Pépin apprenticed

- La Rotonde, 105, boulevard du Montparnasse (6th)—he sometimes saw Sartre, Beauvoir, and Camus while working at this grand café

- Hôtel de Matignon, 57, rue de Varenne (7th)—Pépin served as personal chef to three prime ministers, including Charles de Gaulle, at their official residence here

Pierre-Léon Poilâne (1909-1993)

This late *boulanger's* bread recipe might not be to everyone's liking, but it's pretty impressive that enthusiasts include chefs Ina Garten, Alice Waters, and David Leibovitz. From a family of middle-class farmers in Normandy, Poilâne had to shelve dreams of becoming an architect since funds for education weren't available. An interest in wood-fired ovens led to apprenticeships at bakeries around France. But this young baker wanted to make something quite different from the white-flour baguettes which had become popular after World War I. Remembering the bread of his childhood, he decided to mill flour the old-fashioned way between two stones, mix in his homegrown starter with sea salt, and cook the rounded *miche* in a wood-fired stove. After buying a bakery in the sixth arrondissement, the twenty-three-year-old Poilâne had an oven built in the stone basement according to his specifications. Once he had finished baking for the day, he peddled his wares at local bistros while his wife stayed at the shop as cashier. At the time the sixth arrondissement was heavily populated by poor, young people. Instead of offering them credit, Poilâne traded a loaf for a song about bread, for graffiti praising his product, or for an artwork featuring his bakery. Even today, some of the paintings line the walls of the bakery's offices. Many of Pierre's ways of doing things remain as well. Bakers still use the original starter and, instead of written recipes or oven thermostats, rely on their five senses to produce the bread. Since Poilâne's death in 1993, his family continues to run the business at various Parisian locales.

Addresses for Poilâne

- 8, rue du Cherche-Midi (6th)—site of the original and current bakery

- Au Sauvignon, 80, rue des Saints-Pères (7th)—his first slices of bread were served at this nearby wine bar, still in operation

- Cimetière Bois Tardieu de Clamart, 26, avenue du Bois Tardieu—Poilâne is buried in this cemetery about forty minutes southwest of Paris

Joël Robuchon (1945-2018)

How many superlatives can one man receive? "Chef of the century," "the pope of chefs," "the greatest chef in the world." As a twelve-year-old seminarian, Robuchon was assigned to help out in the kitchen. Deciding that cooking—not the priesthood—was his true calling, he apprenticed in his hometown of Poitiers. In his early twenties he traveled around France discovering regional foods and the delicate dishes of Nouvelle Cuisine. An acknowledgement of the twenty-nine-year-old Robuchon's expertise came when he became head chef at a Paris hotel's restaurant—serving a thousand meals daily. A mere two years later he received the title *Meilleur Ouvrier de France*, France's Best Worker. In 1981 he opened Café Jamin in the 16th which earned Michelin guidebook's three-star rating by 1984. His informal approach, open-mindedness, and creativity won him international recognition, his restaurant becoming the site of gastronomic pilgrimage. But Robuchon was no food snob. His knowledge of classic French cooking combined with regional dishes excited the culinary world: "You don't need expensive or exotic ingredients to create a great cuisine." By the end of the '80s, the Robuchon restaurant empire stretched from Tokyo to New York. Still, he kept his priorities straight. Even though his 1994 Restaurant Joël Robuchon was named "best in the world" by the *International Herald Tribune*, he closed it the following year, having seen too many chefs burn out or die in the business. At age fifty, retired as head chef, Robuchon began a decade-long hosting of his TV show, *Bon appétit bien sûr*. After his death from pancreatic cancer, chefs from around the world attended his funeral.

Addresses for Robuchon

- Hôtel Concorde Lafayette, currently the Hyatt Regency Paris Étoile, 3, place du Général Koenig (17th)—in 1974 Robuchon was named head chef at this hotel's restaurant

- Hôtel Nikko, now Hôtel Novotel Paris Centre Tour Eiffel, 61, quai de Grenelle (15th)—in 1978 he got his first two Michelin stars working here

- Café Jamin, 32, rue de Longchamp (16th)—Robuchon's own restaurant, which opened in 1981, featured excellent food in a relaxed atmosphere

- Restaurant Joël Robuchon, 59, avenue Raymond-Poincaré (16th)—his well-received restaurant was only in business one year

- L'Atelier de Joël Robuchon, 5, rue de Montalembert (7th)—in 2003 he opened this informal bistro in the Hôtel du Pont Royal (and other similar establishments around the world) to make good food sociable and accessible

Chapter 9

Composers, Musicians, and Singers

OVER THE YEARS SINCE the nineteenth century France has definitely left its mark on the world of music. You need only to recall famous classical composers such as Berlioz, Bizet, Debussy, and Ravel. Even popular French singers have had long careers performing on the international stage...Aznavour, Chevalier, and Piaf, for example. You'll read about all of them here, of course, and may even discover several names which are new to you. Two remarkable figures who are in a class by themselves appear in this chapter. For one, there's the incomparable Nadia Boulanger, revered teacher of Aaron Copland, Quincy Jones, and a host of other big-time musicians. And the supremely talented "grandfather of jazz violinists" Stéphane Grappelli could not be omitted from the list. So, enjoy this look at thirteen famous French people in the field of music.

Charles Aznavour (1924-2018)

Sometimes critics really miss the boat. Hard to imagine that, after one reviewer described Aznavour as having "odd looks and an unappealing voice," the singer would go on to become France's answer to Frank Sinatra. In a career that lasted over seventy years, the diminutive "petit Charles" recorded and wrote thousands of songs. He was born in Paris into the Aznavourian family who had immigrated from the Republic of Georgia. His father, also a singer, earned a living running the restaurant Le Caucase where he served Russian meals and often treated penniless fellow Armenians. After dropping out of school at age nine, the boy enrolled in acting and dancing classes at l'École des enfants du spectacle. An early nightclub act with another performer introduced him to singing and songwriting. Soon a protégé of Édith Piaf, Aznavour often opened for the renowned singer and followed her advice in ways to improve his singing style. During the Second World War he and his family risked their own lives hiding and rescuing Jews and others persecuted by the Nazis; decades later, he and his sister Aïda would be presented with the Raoul Wallenberg Award for their efforts. By the early 1960s Aznavour had achieved such popularity in France that he took his act on a world tour performing such great hits as "Et pourtant" and "For Me Formidable." Despite his advancing age and a very long career, Aznavour was still booking concerts until the end of his life. In 2017 the singer received a star on the Hollywood Walk of Fame.

Addresses for Aznavour

- Clinique Tarnier, 89, rue d'Assas (6th)—Aznavour was born in this hospital now an annex of the Hôpital Cochin

- 36, rue Monsieur-le-Prince (6th)—he first lived here with his parents; a memorial plaque marks the building

- 5, rue Champollion and 23, rue de la Huchette (both in the 5th)—former locations of the Aznavour family restaurants, Le Caucase and Le Caucase Bis; the latter address now the site of the Théâtre de la Huchette

- 25, rue du Cardinal-Lemoine (5th)—his father then became manager of a café at this address; the family lived in a studio upstairs

- l'École des enfants du spectacle, 24, rue du Cardinal-Lemoine (5th)—at nine Aznavour enrolled in this part-time performing arts school across from his home

- 22, rue de Navarin (9th)—as a teenager he lived with his family at this address which became a safe haven for Jews and others hunted by the Nazis in WWII

- Moulin Rouge, 82, boulevard de Clichy (18th)—early in his career Aznavour often opened for Edith Piaf at this cabaret

- L'Olympia, 28, boulevard des Capucines (9th)—in 1958 he starred at the famed concert hall

- L'Alhambra-Maurice Chevalier, 50, rue de Malte (11th)—he had a triumphant performance at this former music hall in December 1960

- Le Petit Pergolèse, 38, rue Pergolèse (16th)—one of Aznavour's favorite restaurants, still in operation

Hector Berlioz (1803-1869)

If his parents had had their way, Berlioz would have followed his father into the medical profession. He did, in fact, finish med school only to abandon it for his true passion: music. As a boy in the southeastern département of Isère, Berlioz was mainly schooled by his father. He took flute, guitar, and voice lessons, never studying the piano which he believed saved him "from the lure of conventional harmonies." In September 1821 the young Berlioz arrived in Paris to study medicine, but, ironically, an ample allowance from home gave him the means to become enamored of opera. A short while after earning his medical degree in 1824, Berlioz took courses at the Paris conservatory. On his fifth try in 1830, solely to try to convince his father of his talent, he won the school's premier prize, the Prix de Rome. Two years later he performed a successful concert which attracted Chopin, Liszt, and Paganini as well as Victor Hugo and George Sand. Around the same time Berlioz fell in love with Shakespeare's plays, becoming obsessed with Harriet Smithson as Ophelia in *Hamlet*. The Irish actress, who inspired his "Symphonie fantastique," became his wife in 1833 and the mother of their son Louis, but the marriage didn't last. Berlioz soon began a relationship with soprano Marie Recio whom he married following Smithson's death in 1854. Because his works achieved only moderate success, Berlioz turned his attention to writing articles on music and conducting symphonies throughout Europe. In 1856 he started writing "Les Troyens," an ambitious five-act opera which he never saw performed in its entirety.

Addresses for Berlioz

- 104, (the number no longer exists) rue Saint-Jacques (5th)— Berlioz first lived here with his cousin, also a medical student, before moving to #71 on the same street

- Conservatoire de Paris, 209, rue Jean Jaurès (19th)—in 1826 he began music studies, winning the Prix de Rome on his fifth attempt

- 22, rue du Mont-Cenis, then called the rue Saint-Denis (18th)— he and his wife lived at this location for two years; a plaque marks the building

- 31, rue de Londres (9th)—from 1837 to 1844 he had an apartment here

- 41, rue de Provence (9th)—Berlioz lived for a while at Marie Recio's place

- 15, rue de la Rochefoucault (9th)—the couple then spent a year at this address until 1849

- 19, rue de Boursault (17th)—they lived at this location before spending seven months at 17, rue de Vintimille (9th)

- 4, rue de Calais (9th)—the apartment where Berlioz died at age sixty-five

- Église de la Trinité, place Estienne d'Orves (9th)—his funeral was held at this church

- Cimetière de Montmartre, 20, avenue Rachel (18th)—his grave is next to his two wives in division 20

Georges Bizet (1838-1875)

Disappointed by the poor reaction to *Carmen* on opening night, Bizet described his opera as a "hopeless flop." Sadly, the composer never lived to see its worldwide popularity in the classical canon. A child prodigy, he took piano lessons from his mother before receiving special permission to attend the Paris conservatory before the age of ten. His delightful "Symphony in C Major," composed at seventeen, was eventually used to accompany a Balanchine ballet. After being awarded the conservatory's Prix de Rome, Bizet spent several years in the Italian capital at the French Académie which he termed "a paradise." At a dinner party in Paris in May 1861 he impressed Franz Liszt by sight-reading one of the Hungarian composer's most difficult piano pieces, prompting him to call the twenty-two-year-old Bizet one of "the boldest and most brilliant" pianists in Europe. In June 1872 Bizet was commissioned to compose a piece based on Prosper Mérimée's short novel *Carmen*. While the composer described his opera as "all clarity and vivacity, full of color and melody," its premiere in March 1875 shocked audiences with its risqué themes of betrayal and murder. Critics also described it as vulgar and immoral. Later in November of that same year Bizet's "L'Arlésienne," first composed as background music for a play by Daudet, achieved instant success. Debilitated by overwork and smoking, he died from heart problems at thirty-six. On the night of his funeral the press, which had nearly universally condemned the piece three months earlier, reacted to a special performance of *Carmen* by declaring Bizet a master.

Addresses for Bizet

- 26, rue de la Tour-d'Auvergne (9th)—Bizet was born at this address

- Conservatoire de Paris, 209, rue Jean Jaurès (19th)—two weeks before his tenth birthday he entered the conservatory, remaining at the school from 1848 to 1857

- Théâtre Lyrique, 72, boulevard du Temple, now 10, place de la République (11th)—his opera *Les Pêcheurs de Perles* was an initial failure at this theater in 1863; *La Jolie Fille de Perth* was hailed as a masterpiece at the same venue four years later

- Hôtel Halévy, 22, rue de Douai (9th)—this historical monument is the mansion where Bizet lived from 1869 until his death; a memorial plaque can be found on the building

- Théâtre National de l'Opéra Comique, 1, place Boieldieu (2nd)— *Carmen* first shocked audiences and displeased critics at this theater

- 5, rue Ivan Tourguéniev, Bougival—Bizet rented a country home on the Seine at this location west of Paris where he died

- Église de la Sainte-Trinité, place Estienne d'Orves (9th)—4,000 people attended his funeral at this church

- Cimetière du Père Lachaise, 16, rue du Repos (20th)—Bizet is interred in division 68 of this cemetery

- Opéra Garnier, place de l'Opéra (9th)—in 1947 George Balanchine premiered Bizet's "Symphony in C" as a ballet at this opera house

Nadia Boulanger (1887-1979)

To many outsiders, Quincy Jones, Aaron Copland, and Yehudi Menuhin are much more famous in the world of music than the French woman who taught them. But those "in the know" hold Mademoiselle Boulanger in very high esteem; one musician, in fact, called her "the most influential teacher since Socrates." No small praise indeed. But Boulanger was also a respected pianist, organist, conductor, and composer—even though she found her own compositions "useless." Born in Paris to a Russian mother and a musician who was a voice teacher at the Conservatory, Nadia was frightened by music as a young child. By age five, however, she was recreating sounds she heard on the piano. Her father's death when she was thirteen put a financial strain on his widow and two daughters. Four years later Nadia began supporting the family by giving private music lessons at home. In 1907 Boulanger took a job teaching piano at the Conservatoire Femina-Musica and later at the École Normale de musique. Concerts, compositions, and occasional articles on music followed. When the French Music School for Americans opened in 1921 in Fontainebleau, thirty-five miles southeast of Paris, she became a professor of harmony, often inviting her best students, like Copland, for a weekend at her summer residence. Boulanger was the first woman to conduct orchestras in Boston, New York, Philadelphia, and London. A demanding and at times impatient teacher, she lived according to the axiom that "the essential conditions of everything you do must be choice, love, and passion."

Addresses for Boulanger

- Conservatoire de Paris, 209, rue Jean Jaurès (19th)—after entering this school at nine, she studied with Gabriel Fauré and received honors but felt she had no talent in composition; she taught at the school from 1946 to 1957

- 36, rue Ballu (9th)—from the time she was seventeen Boulanger taught music and lived at this address with her mother and sister Lili (also a very talented musician)

- Conservatoire Femina-Musica, rue Jouffroy-d'Abbans (number unknown)—Boulanger was a piano professor at this one-time school

- École normale de musique, 114 bis, boulevard Malesherbes (18th)—she taught a variety of music classes here

- Théâtre des Champs-Élysées, 15, avenue Montaigne (8th)—where she conducted the philharmonic orchestra

- Cimetière de Montmartre, 20, avenue Rachel (18th)—burial place of Nadia, along with her parents and sister in division 33

Georges Brassens (1921-1981)

With his unpolished appearance and gravelly voice, Brassens was not the stereotype of a singer-songwriter, much less an award-winning poet. But for more than thirty years he wrote and recorded over 200 songs and in 1967 received the highest poetry award from the Académie Française. Growing up in a musical family in the Mediterranean city of Sète, he was encouraged to keep writing poems by a high school teacher. After getting expelled from school in 1939, he moved in with his aunt in Paris where he worked at a Renault factory and continued studying poetry at the public library in his spare time. During WWII, the twenty-two-year-old Brassens was forced to make BMW airplane motors in Germany. On leave in March '44 he never went back to the labor camp, hiding out in the modest home of Jeanne Planche, his future lover and biggest fan of his music. In 1951 while hoping to become a poet or a composer, he found employment as a singer but severe stage fright nearly put an early end to his career. At Chez Patachou in Montmartre the following year he dazzled audiences with his simple melodies and subversive lyrics, soon landing contracts with top record producers. His first hit "Gorille" (1952), which made a strong stance against the death penalty, was considered pornographic by French government officials who banned the song for three years. Another hit "Je me suis fait tout petit" ("I Was Laid Low") Brassens wrote for the love of his life, an Estonian woman named Joha Heiman who is buried next to him in Sète.

Addresses for Brassens

- 173, rue d'Alésia (14th)—he first lived in his Aunt Antoinette's boarding house in 1940

- 9, impasse Florimont (14th)—address of Jeanne and Marcel Planche where Brassens stayed from 1944 to '66; a commemorative plaque marks the building

- Le République, once Le Caveau de la République, 1, boulevard Saint-Martin (3rd)—in 1951 Brassens started performing at this club using a borrowed guitar

- Chez Patachou, 13, rue du Mont-Cenis (18th)—the next year the singer impressed audiences at this cabaret

- Salle Pleyel, 252, rue du Faubourg Saint-Honoré (8th)—he recorded "Gorille" here in March 1952

- Les Trois Baudets, 64, boulevard de Clichy (18th)—Brassens played to packed houses here

- Bobino, 20, rue de la Gaîté (14th)—in February of '53 he first performed at his favorite music hall; by October he was the star attraction

- L'Olympia, 28 boulevard des Capucines (9th)—Brassens starred here in 1954

- Hôtel Meridien, 19, rue Émile-Dubois (14th)—for a brief time he had a room at this hotel

- 42, rue Santos-Dumont (15th)—Brassens lived at this address from 1968 to 1981; a park named for him is located nearby

Maurice Chevalier (1888-1972)

The twelve-year-old boy, laughed at for singing off key and paid with a cup of coffee, eventually did pretty well for himself. Through hard work and perseverance, he earned the title of "the most expensive artist in the world." His father abandoned the family early, prompting the boy to apprentice in factory jobs. But the poor street kid never gave up on his dream of becoming a singer. He tried using acrobatics, dance, and salacious humor on stage but gradually refined his act. Beginning in 1908, Chevalier had the good fortune of partnering (professionally and romantically) with two female stars: Fréhel and Mistinguett. From that time he developed a drug habit which would only be broken during his twenty-six months as a prisoner of war during WWI. Out of boredom during that period in Germany, Chevalier learned English from fellow British internees which proved quite an asset in future years. In the 1920s Douglas Fairbanks and Mary Pickford caught Chevalier's performance in an operetta in Paris, paving his way into American movies. Because of the lack of dubbing equipment, the actor had to film both in English and in French. But audiences loved him; and from the start a director noted: "you're sitting on top of the world, Maurice." A confirmed penny-pincher (old habits die hard), Chevalier was a Hollywood star over a nearly forty-year career. He received an honorary Oscar for *Gigi* in 1958. However, like many others of his time, Chevalier was accused of collaboration with the Nazis during WWII but was later acquitted by French courts.

Addresses for Chevalier
- 27 (or #29), rue du Retrait—the actor was born at this address

but the family soon moved to a tiny apartment at 15, rue Julien Lacroix (both in the 20th)

- Casino des Tourelles, formerly at 259, avenue Gambetta (20th)— his first successful singing engagement was here

- 15, rue du Faubourg-du-Temple (11th) and 118, rue du Faubourg-Saint-Martin (10th)—when finances got a bit easier for the family, they moved to apartments at these locations

- La Scala, 13, boulevard de Strasbourg (10th)—this recently reopened venue was a café-concert when Chevalier performed there

- Eldorado, now Le Comédia, 4, boulevard de Strasbourg (10th)— headlining at this spot for two months for 1000 francs a month, he had such stage fright at the premiere that he went on stage drunk but was still triumphant

- Folies-Bergère, 32, rue Richier (9th)—on four separate occasions on this stage he was the dance partner of Mistinguett—the only woman he ever loved

- 18, boulevard de Strasbourg (10th)—he and his mother moved here after his success at the Folies-Bergère

- Café des Ambassadeurs, now Espace Pierre-Cardin, 1, rue Gabriel (8th)—Chevalier spent three summer seasons performing at this location

- La Cigale, 124, boulevard de Rochechouart (18th)—in 1912 he was on stage here

- Casino Montparnasse, once found at 35, rue de la Gaîté (14th) and l'Olympia, 28, boulevard des Capucines (9th)—concert halls where Chevalier took jobs after being released as a prisoner of war

- Casino de Paris, 16, rue de Clichy (9th)—he had many engagements at this venue

- Théâtre Fémina, once found at 90, avenue des Champs-Élysées (8th) and Théâtre Marigny, Carré Marigny (8th)—he and

Mistinguett were much admired at these two theaters

- Théâtre des Bouffes-Parisiens 4, rue Monsigny (2nd)— Fairbanks and Pickford saw his performance in the operetta *Dédé* at this theater

- 83, boulevard des Courcelles (8th)—Chevalier's large apartment during WWII

- 85, rue Ampère (17th)—he also lived on this street though the number is uncertain

- Théâtre des Champs-Élysées, 15, avenue Montaigne (8th)—Chevalier gave his final concert here on October 20, 1968

Claude Debussy (1862-1918)

This innovative, influential composer described himself as "too enamored" of his freedom—which was true in school, music, and in his personal life. His family moved into Paris from the suburbs when he was six. Introduced to the piano by an aunt, he took lessons for a year before entering the conservatory at age ten. In his school years teachers found him intelligent and ingenious yet inattentive and careless; he often arrived late or skipped class altogether. At thirteen he began a four-year stint as an accompanist for a voice class. After falling in love with one of the students, Marie Vasnier, Debussy wrote twenty-seven songs for her during their seven-year relationship. In 1879 Debussy was hired as a resident pianist at the Château de Chenonceau, where he developed a lifelong taste for luxury. While touring Europe as a pianist for a wealthy family, he gained experience and confidence. Failing to win conservatory prizes for a few years, Debussy finally secured the Prix de Rome in 1884. He cut his time short in the Italian capital, however, because he disliked the atmosphere, accommodations, and food, preferring to return to Marie in Paris. The pieces he wrote in Rome were judged "strange, incomprehensible, and impossible to play" by teachers back home. Once he quit the conservatory, Debussy had a series of sometimes overlapping romances, including one with Emma Bardac who gave birth to his daughter. His orchestral masterpiece "Prélude à l'après-midi d'un faune" (1894) brought him European recognition. Likewise, his only opera *Pelléas et Mélisande* (1902) made him famous abroad. Debussy died of cancer at age fifty-five.

Addresses for Debussy

- 11, rue de Vintimille (9th)—the family first lived at this address in Paris before moving to 69, rue Saint-Honoré (1st)

- 59 bis, rue Pigalle (9th)—his mother had a tiny apartment with her four children while the father was incarcerated for a year

- Conservatoire de Paris, 209, rue Jean Jaurès (19th)—at age ten he entered the conservatory

- 13, rue Clapeyron (8th)—the family lived here after the father was released from prison in 1874

- rue Taitbout, no number found (9th)—Debussy worked as an accompanist for Marie Moreau-Sainti's singing class for four years

- 42, rue de Londres (8th)—he lived with Gaby Dupont for nearly ten years at this address

- Salle Favart, officially Théâtre National de l'Opéra Comique, 1, place Boieldieu (2nd)— Debussy's opera premiered here on April 30, 1902

- 80, avenue du Bois de Boulogne, now 23, square Avenue Foch (16th)—his home with Emma from 1905 until the end of his life; a memorial plaque is on the main doorway

- Cimetière de Passy, 2, rue du Commandant Scholesing (16th)— Debussy is buried in division 14 of this cemetery

Serge Gainsbourg (1928-1991)

This legendary singer-songwriter has similarities with Bob Dylan. Both had Russian Jewish ancestors; both performed using pseudonyms; and both wrote songs that influenced generations. One major difference is that Lucien Ginsburg grew up in occupied France. At the age of eleven the shy boy and his family were forced to wear the discriminating yellow star. Using false papers to escape the Nazis, the Ginsburgs moved four hours south to Limoges. Returning to Paris after Liberation, the teenager didn't pass the exams at the end of high school. He took a series of art classes, seriously hoping to become a painter. Having an appreciation for classical music, he also concentrated on playing the piano. In 1954 after filling in for his father as a pianist, he fell upon his future calling in music. Three years later he settled on his stage name: Serge to indicate his Russian roots and Gainsbourg to honor his favorite painter Thomas Gainsborough. An early hit song describing the monotonous life of a métro ticket puncher is the reason fans still leave subway tickets on his grave. After hearing the provocative lyrics of musician Boris Vian, Gainsbourg discovered his own path. He went on to write controversial, often sexually explicit tunes such as "Je t'aime moi non plus" and "Les Sucettes" which by being censored or banned gave him international publicity. Gainsbourg varied his musical style greatly during his career, producing over 550 songs. A chain smoker, in later years he often appeared at venues inebriated with a glass in hand. At Gainsbourg's death President Mitterrand praised the singer once called "a walking pollution" by journalists, saying that "he elevated song to the level of art."

Addresses for Gainsbourg

- Hôtel Dieu [now the Hôpitaux Universitaires Paris Centre], 1, place du Parvis-Notre-Dame (4th)—Lucien Ginsburg was born in this hospital

- 35, rue de la Chine (20th)—a family residence including another at 11 bis, rue Chaptal (9th) where he lived from age four to nineteen; there's a memorial plaque at the second location

- 55, avenue Bugeaud (16th)—upon their return from Limoges the family bought an apartment at this address

- Lycée Condorcet, 8, rue du Havre (9th)—his grades were a

disaster except for history and English; he often skipped class and failed the *bac* at the end of high school

- Académie de Montmartre, 104, boulevard de Clichy (18th)—he took art courses and met his first wife here

- Schola Cantorum, 269, rue Saint-Jacques (5th)—in 1952 he and his wife Elizabeth had a room at this conservatory

- Le Cabaret Madame Arthur, 75, rue des Martyrs (18th)—the twenty-six-year-old Gainsbourg first took the stage here while replacing his father as a pianist in 1954

- Milord l'Arsouille, 5, rue de Beaujolais (1st)—he caught the act of Boris Vian and eventually performed his own songs at this former cabaret

- 33, rue Verneuil (7th)—in 1962 he partied with Juliette Greco at her apartment then wrote the song *La Javanaise* for her

- Raspoutine, 58, rue de Bassano (8th)—Russian restaurant where Gainsbourg took Jane Birkin on their first date

- L'Hôtel, 13, rue des Beaux-Arts (6th)—Gainsbourg composed the album *Histoire de Melody* while living with Birkin for a year at this hotel with an unoriginal name

- Le Bistrot de Paris, 33, rue de Lille (7th)—a regular guest, supposedly at his favorite table 46, he had a glass of port here on the night he died

- 5 bis, rue de Verneuil (6th)—where he lived from 1969 until his death; fans still put notes or drawings on the building which his daughter Charlotte would like to turn into a museum

- Cimetière du Montparnasse, 3, boulevard Edgar Quinet (14th)— Gainsbourg is buried in the 1st division of this cemetery

Stéphane Grappelli (1908-1997)

Although referred to as "the grandfather of jazz violinists," let's just say that his tone, technique, and improvising skills made him one of the greats. Following his mother's death when he was four, his father was drafted into the Italian army during WWI. Entrusted to the care of his dance teacher Isadora Duncan who soon left for the U.S., Grappelli was sent to "an abominable" orphanage where there was little to eat. After the war, his father pawned a suit to buy the boy a three-fourth-size violin which he learned to play by watching others before studying at the conservatory. At twelve he began busking on the streets to bring home a few coins. Three years later, a strolling mandolin player offered him a job in a Montmartre cinema's pit orchestra, where they performed everything from ragtime to Mozart. As part of a jazz group with celebrated guitarist Django Reinhardt, Grappelli felt that musically speaking "my life started." In 1934 the duo founded the Quintette du Hot Club de France, one of the first all-string jazz bands. While at a gig in London, Grappelli fell ill, forcing him to spend WWII in England. Over a sixty-year career he made hundreds of recordings with musicians as diverse as Duke Ellington, Paul Simon, Yo-Yo Ma, and Oscar Peterson. Between 1972 and '76, he recorded three albums with classical violinist Yehudi Menuhin who said about Grappelli: "he is a man I envy almost as much I love him." In 1983 he was inducted into Down Beat magazine's Jazz Hall of Fame and later received a Grammy Lifetime Achievement Award.

Addresses for Grappelli

- Hôpital Lariboisière-Fernand Widal, 2, rue Ambroise-Paré (10th)—Grappelli was born at this hospital

- 28, rue de Montholon (9th)—until the death of his mother, he lived at this address then moved with his father to the seventh floor at 59 bis, rue [Marguerite] de Rochechouart (9th)

- Conservatoire de Paris, 209, rue Jean Jaurès (19th)—at twelve he entered the conservatory and first heard a jazz band at a nearby dance hall

- [Paris Marriott Opéra] Ambassador Hotel, 16, boulevard Haussmann (9th)—Grappelli was member of this hotel's orchestra

- La Croix du Sud, once found at 3. boulevard du Montparnasse

(6th)—Reinhardt and Grappelli met performing jazz at this chic club

- Hôtel Claridge, 37, rue François 1er (8th)—the Quintette was formed after backstage jams at a "thé dansant" at this hotel

- La Grosse Pomme, 73, rue Jean-Baptiste Pigalle (9th)—jazz singer Adelaide Hall's former club where the Quintette was a house band in 1937

- 26, rue Norvins (18th)—the band also regularly performed at the Perriers' R-26 salon

- 87, rue de Dunkerque (9th)—a plaque marks the building where Grappelli lived on the sixth floor for the last thirty years of his life

- Cimetière du Père Lachaise, 16, rue du Repos (20th)—he is interred in division 87, case 417 of this cemetery's columbarium

Johnny Hallyday (1943-2017)

USA Today once mocked Hallyday as being "the biggest rock star you never heard of." But this best-selling singer was nothing less than a cultural icon in his home country. The hip-swiveling "French Elvis," who made eighty-two albums over his long career, dabbled in all genres—from blues to country. He was best known, however, as the guy who brought rock 'n' roll to France. Born Jean-Philippe Smet, he had a rough start in life after his Belgian father abandoned him and his mother. Fortunately, a substitute father came along in the form of a cousin's husband, an entertainer from Oklahoma who performed as Lee Halliday. Lee called the boy "Johnny" and introduced him to American music. When the fourteen-year-old Johnny discovered Elvis, he decided his future was to become a rocker. Three years later his first record came out with his stage name incorrectly spelled as "Hallyday" on the label. By eighteen, he had recorded dozens of songs and had already sold over 1.5 million records. Over the years he collaborated with singers like Aznavour, Piaf, and Sylvie Vartan, who became his first wife. Although Hallyday set records for attendance at his concerts at home, he was never able to crack the American market. Extremely wealthy, he maintained a "flamboyant lifestyle," buying homes in affluent areas from Gstaad, Switzerland, to Saint-Bart's in the Caribbean. When French officials hounded him for millions in back taxes, Hallyday moved his family to Pacific Palisades, California. On the day of his funeral, nearly a million people lined the Champs-Élysées to pay him tribute.

Addresses for Hallyday

- Villa Marie-Louise, 3, Cité Malesherbes (9th)—he was born at this former maternity hospital

- Église de la Sainte-Trinité, place Estienne d'Orves (9th)—the church where he was baptized

- 13, rue de la Tour-des-Dames (9th)—during the mid-1950s he lived at this address

- Golf-Drouot, 2, rue Drouot (9th)—the first rock discothèque in France which Hallyday frequented along with many other early rockers

- L'Alhambra, 50, rue de Malte (11th)—the public was divided during his three weeks at this former music hall—adults booed and young people loved him

- L'Olympia, 28, boulevard des Capucines (8th)—in 1961 he was the first of his generation to star at the famous concert hall, introducing the twist to the French audience; he would perform at the venue many times throughout his career

- Église de la Madeleine, place de la Madeleine (8th)—Hallyday's funeral took place at this church before his burial in Saint Bart's

Édith Piaf (1915-1963)

The world-famous *chanteuse* once stated: "I want to make people cry even when they don't understand my words"…and hit songs like *La Vie en Rose* and *Non, Je Ne Regrette Rien* had just that touching quality. She was born Édith Giovanna Gassion in the Belleville section of Paris. Her life, as portrayed in print and films, was filled with tragedy.

Just an infant, Édith was abandoned by her mother and raised by her paternal grandmother who ran a brothel in Normandy. At seventeen, while singing on the streets of Montmartre, she fell in love—and soon gave birth to a baby daughter who died of meningitis at age two. Her professional break came when she was discovered by Louis Leplée, owner of a nightclub off the Champs-Élysées. He greatly influenced her career: giving the petite twenty-year-old Gassion the nickname Môme Piaf (slang for "little sparrow"), teaching her stage presence, as well as having her dress in her trademark black attire. Thus began a whirlwind of recordings, acting jobs, as well as appearances in the U.S. on *The Ed Sullivan Show* and concerts at Carnegie Hall. Following World War II she was accused of collaborating with the Nazis but was later cleared of charges. Piaf had many romantic relationships, including with singer/actor Yves Montand. The love of her life, however, was married boxer Marcel Cerdan, who perished in a plane crash in 1949. A series of automobile accidents caused injuries exacerbating Piaf's physical pain and addiction to alcohol and medications. She died of liver cancer at age forty-seven.

Addresses for Piaf

- Hôpital Tenon, 4, rue Chine (20th)—hospital where both Édith and her daughter were born

- 72, rue de Belleville (20th)—the historical plaque above the door notes that her mother gave birth to her on the steps outside, which is no doubt apocryphal

- Grand Hôtel de Clermont, 18, rue Veron (18th)—she took a room in this hotel while performing as a young street singer in Montmartre

- Le Gerny's, 54, rue Pierre Charron (8th)—one-time nightclub where Louis Leplée gave Piaf her nickname and her big break into show business

- L'Olympia, 28, boulevard des Capucines (9th)—her series of performances at this concert hall solidified her fame

- L'Étoile de Kléber, 4, rue Paul Valéry (16th)—during World War II Piaf took a room above this former brothel/nightclub close to Gestapo headquarters

- 45, rue de Chézy and 23, rue Édouard Nortier—two addresses where she once lived in Neuilly-sur-Seine, just west of Paris near the Bois de Boulogne

- 67, boulevard Lannes (16th)— a white historical plaque notes Piaf's residence for the last ten years of her life

- Cimetière du Père Lachaise, 16, rue du Repos (20th)—Piaf is interred in division 97 of this cemetery along with her father, daughter, and her second husband Théo Lamboukas Sarapo; it has been reported that as many as 100,000 people showed up at her burial

- Musée Édith Piaf, 5, rue Crespin du Gast (11th)—a two-room museum dedicated to the singer can be found at this address near Père Lachaise Cemetery

Maurice Ravel (1875-1937)

Being the twice-expelled student from the Paris Conservatory who became a master of orchestration and an internationally admired composer pretty much sums up Ravel. The family moved from a southwestern town near Biarritz to the capital when he was an infant. By all accounts he had a happy childhood, mainly homeschooled by music-loving parents who encouraged his piano lessons at age seven. After entering the conservatory in 1889, he won a piano competition at sixteen but was far from a star student. Often disinterested and rebellious, Ravel had a fan in one of his teachers, Gabriel Fauré, but was generally not well regarded by the music faculty. Meanwhile, his growing reputation as a musician in the public eye resulted in the so-called "affaire Ravel"—an uproar which developed when he was rejected for the fifth time for the school's Prix de Rome. Outside of class he and some raucous young friends formed "Les Apaches," an avant-garde group who discussed music and first heard Ravel's piano piece "Jeux d'eau." Having abandoned the conservatory for good in 1903, Ravel began his slow, painstaking style of writing for piano before arranging for full orchestra. He served courageously as a military truck driver during WWI before returning to composition. His output includes very difficult piano music, operas, ballets, and chamber music—but no symphonies or church music. Interestingly, he held his most famous work in very low regard: "I've written only one masterpiece—'Boléro.' Unfortunately, there's no music in it." Quite sensitive about his small stature (five feet), he was also secretive about his personal life which remains a mystery to this day.

Addresses for Ravel

- 40, rue des Martyrs (9ᵗʰ)—for several years the Ravel family lived near place Pigalle before moving a short distance away in 1880 to 29, rue Victor-Massé, then the rue de Laval (9ᵗʰ)

- 73, rue Jean-Baptiste-Pigalle (9ᵗʰ)—in 1886 they lived on fifth floor here and he wrote his first compositions

- Conservatoire de Paris, 209, rue Jean Jaurès (19ᵗʰ)—at fourteen Ravel entered this conservatory

- 15, rue Lagrange (5ᵗʰ)—in 1896 the family moved to the Left Bank for three years

- 7, rue Fromentin (9ᵗʰ)—when Ravel was twenty-four the family lived at this address

- Nouveau Théâtre, now the Théâtre de Paris, 15, rue Blanche (9ᵗʰ)—he made his conducting début with "Shéhérazade," getting a hostile critical reception

- 40 bis, rue de Douai (9ᵗʰ)—the family lived here for a few months before moving to 19, boulevard Pereire (17ᵗʰ) near his father and brother's engineering jobs, then to 11, rue Louis Rouquier (previously the rue Chevallier) in Levallois just outside the city limits

- 4, avenue Carnot (17ᵗʰ)—after the father's death, the mother and two sons moved to this "delicious apartment;" a memorial plaque is on the building

- Théâtre des Champs-Élysées, 15, avenue Montaigne (8th)—his ballet *Le Tombeau de Couperin* was staged at this theater in November 1920 and *La Valse* that December
- Opéra Garnier, place de l'Opéra (9th)—in 1921 *Daphnis et Chloé* and *L'Heure espagnole* were revived at this opera house
- Cimetière de Levallois-Perret, 101, rue Baudin—he is buried with his family at this cemetery

Érik Satie (1866-1925)

This eccentric composer, known as the "velvet gentlemen" because of his seven identical velour suits, often composed pieces in a notebook while walking down the streets of Paris at night. Once during the WWI bombing of the city he even found inspiration for his work lying at the foot of the obelisk at place de la Concorde. Named Éric at his birth in the Norman city of Honfleur, he took music lessons early, entering the conservatory in the capital in 1879. Judged to be lazy and without talent by most of his professors, Satie nevertheless published compositions as a teenager. In 1887 while working as a pianist in local cabarets, he met fellow musician Debussy who would host Satie for lunch on Fridays. The following year he published two of his three works for piano "Gymnopédies." During a religious period as the official composer at a church, Satie fell madly in love with artist Suzanne Valadon who ended their relationship five months later. Preferring the term *phonometrician* ("one who measures sound") to musician, Satie composed spare, unconventional pieces in reaction to the heavy nineteenth-century "salon music," writing copious remarks on the scores of his compositions. By the end of the 1890s he felt the need to "withdraw completely" from the bohemian life in Paris, moving to the southern suburb of Arcueil. In over twenty-five years at that location, he lived as a hoarder in squalor and chaos…with two grand pianos placed one on top of the other. A heavy drinker, Satie died of cirrhosis of the liver at age fifty-nine.

Addresses for Satie

- Conservatoire de Paris, 209, rue Jean Jaurès (19th)—as a teenager

Satie took classes at the conservatory where one teacher told him his talent was in composition

- 50, rue Condorcet (9th)—at age twenty-one he moved from home to this address where he lived a reckless, bohemian life

- Le Chat Noir, 12, rue de Laval, now rue Victor-Massé (9th)—in 1888 while earning a living as a pianist at this cabaret, he introduced himself as a "gymnopedist"—a name that would figure in the title of three of his pieces for piano

- 6, rue Cortot (18th)—between 1890 and 1898 he rented two different apartments here—the last two years in a tiny closet-like space; a memorial plaque marks the building

- 22, rue de la Boétie (8th)—around 1900 Satie often worked at his friend Henry Pacory's place

- 22 (now #34), rue Cauchy, Arcueil—for twenty-seven years he lived just across the southern border of Paris, often composing at the bistro then found below his room

- Chez la Mère Tulard, rue Émile-Raspail (no number), Arcueil— Satie often ate and wrote pieces at this former restaurant

- Schola Cantorum, 269, rue Saint-Jacques (5th)—from October 1905 to '08 he studied counterpoint here where he was a respected student

- Théâtre du Châtelet, 2, rue Édouard Colonne (1st)—Cocteau's scenario *Parade*, staged through the help of Satie and Picasso, was performed by the Ballets Russes at this theater in 1917

- Cimetière d'Arcueil, 15, avenue Paul Vaillant Couturier—Satie is buried in this cemetery

Chapter 10

Fashion Designers

THE FRENCH EXCEL IN many disparate areas including literature, the fine arts, music, science, and cuisine. But it seems that the fashion and perfume industries immediately spring to mind whenever many people think of France. And for good reason. The country is now—and has long been—the epitome of style, attracting notice and admiration from Cheapos as well as Snobs. In the domain of *haute couture*, clothing and fragrances from the companies of such superstars as Coco Chanel, Christian Dior, Hubert de Givenchy, Yves Saint-Laurent, and Louis Vuitton enjoy a sterling reputation and figure prominently on the world stage. In this chapter you'll read about the designers who created those very houses. And along the way you might just discover some new names like Jacques Fath and Paul Poiret who played an important part in French fashion history.

Coco Chanel (1883-1971)

When we hear the name Chanel, we think women's suits, the "little black dress," handbags, and perfumes, right? A Nazi spy? Not so much. But according to recently declassified documents, the fashion house's creator was just that. Born poor in Saumur southwest of Paris, Gabrielle Bonheur Chanel offered several versions of her past. The truth seems to be that after her mother died when she was twelve, she and her sisters were placed in an orphanage. One bright spot is that the future designer learned to sew during her six years there. Early affairs with wealthy men provided her with the funds to open a hat shop in Paris. Subsequently, highly successful boutiques in the seaside towns of Deauville and Biarritz encouraged the expansion of her line to women's clothing. In 1919 Chanel opened a shop in the French capital, selling clothes and eventually jewelry and perfume. She designed costumes for French performing arts—even for MGM studios in Hollywood, a town she called "the capital of bad taste." By 1935 Chanel employed over 4,000 people; at the same time she developed a drug habit which continued for the rest of her life. Her views against Jews, immigrants, and gays gave her an affinity with Nazis occupying France during World War II and drove her to become one of their agents. Winston Churchill's intervention in the case—due to Chanel's ability to link royal family members and high-ranking British officials to the Germans—saved her from being jailed.

Addresses for Chanel

- 21, rue Cambon (1st)—site of Chanel Modes, her first hat shop; she maintained an apartment on the top floor at #31 on the same street which was (and still is) the address of her fashion boutique

- Hôtel Ritz, 15, place Vendôme (1st)—Chanel maintained suite #302 at the luxury hotel for 34 years

- Théâtre des Champs-Élysées, 15, avenue Montaigne (8th)—she designed costumes for a play at this theater

- Le Train Bleu, place Louis-Armand (12th)—in the early 1920s Chanel was a regular customer at this luxury restaurant inside the Gare de Lyon; she also frequented Angelina, a fashionable tearoom at 226, rue de Rivoli (1st). (Read about both locations in Chapter 2)

- Musée des Arts Décoratifs, 107, rue de Rivoli (1st)—some of Chanel's creations can be viewed at this museum as well as at the Palais Galliera, 10, avenue Pierre-1er-de-Serbie (16th); both are discussed in Chapter 3

- Église de la Madeleine, place de la Madeleine (8th)—site of Chanel's funeral before her burial in Lausanne, Switzerland Grand Palais, 3, avenue du Général Eisenhower (8th)—twice-a-year contemporary Chanel collections are shown during Paris Fashion Week at this exhibition hall

Christian Dior (1905-1957)

Even as a child, Dior said he was amused by anything "sparkling, elaborate, flowery, or frivolous." It stands to reason then that the artistically inclined boy would gravitate toward fashion design rather than diplomacy as his parents had hoped. During his youth, after his wealthy family moved to Paris from Normandy, he began selling sketches on the street. His parents strongly discouraged these creative pursuits in favor of the study of political science. They were mortified for the Dior name when their son opened a small art gallery and went on to pursue his dream of working in fashion. Employment with designer Robert Piguet taught him "the virtues of simplicity through which true elegance must come." Dior started his own company at the end of 1946, launching the next spring what would become one of the world's top brands of haute couture. But success didn't come easy. Termed the "New Look" by *Harper's Bazaar* magazine, the designs used voluminous amounts of fabric which were criticized by French women used to scrimping every bit of cloth during the rationing of World War II. His rival Coco Chanel ridiculed the designer, saying he "upholsters women." Others, however, saw the extravagant, luxurious clothing as an expression of liberty. Supporters like Princess Margaret, Rita Hayworth, and Marilyn Monroe began buying his fashions. Soon, perfumes, furs, and stockings were added to the collection. Unfortunately, the designer died at age fifty-two under mysterious circumstances just ten years after his business began. His flourishing Maison Dior lives on.

Addresses for Dior

- Collège Stanislas, 22, rue Notre-Dame-des-Champs (6th)—he attended this prestigious private school

- Science Po, 27, rue Saint-Guillaume (7th)—location of the head office and library of the school where Dior studied political science for three years to please his parents
- 10, rue Royale (8th)—address of his one-time apartment near the place de la Concorde; the current site of a Dior boutique is found at #25 on the same street
- 30, avenue Montaigne (8th)—the Dior flagship store is located here
- Musée des Arts Décoratifs, 107, rue de Rivoli (1st)—this museum houses the works of many fashion designers including Dior as does the Palais Galliera, 10, avenue Pierre-1er-de-Serbie (16th)

Jacques Fath (1912-1954)

If you're asking yourself "Jacques who?" about now, I'm sure you're not alone. In the post-WWII era, though, along with Dior and Balmain, Fath was a dominant influence in haute couture. As a boy growing up northwest of Paris, he loved creating costumes for himself. His insurance broker father succeeded in having him study business and bookkeeping—which would come in handy later on. After a brief foray into the corporate world, Fath had an apprenticeship at a fashion house. Then in 1937, the young, self-taught designer opened a small shop in the capital. During the gasoline rationing of WWII, he created full, practical skirts to liberate women's movements as they traveled via bicycle. Although his talent wasn't immediately appreciated by prominent fashion magazines, within ten years his young chic style, full of color and movement, really took off. His collection attracted actresses Ava Gardner, Rita Hayworth, and Greta Garbo. Even magazines like *Harper's Bazaar* began noticing that Fath "makes you look like you have sex appeal." A handsome, charming couple, he and his wife, one of his models, became like royalty, throwing huge, extravagant parties and appearing in press photographs. Fath understood using his personal appeal for marketing; and, as one biographer wrote, "he channeled his temperament into his designs." He also wasn't shy about accepting Nazi clientele but never suffered the consequences. In 1953 the designer launched his Université line of ready-to-wear clothing for the American market which earned the title of "wearable glamor." At the height of his glory Fath died of leukemia at age forty-two.

Addresses for Fath

- 32, rue La Boétie (8th)—at twenty-five he opened his two-room shop with a handful of employees

- 39, avenue Pierre-1er-de-Serbie (8th)—after a time on the rue François 1er, the Maison Fath settled here

- Château de Corbeville, 7, Chemin de la Ménagerie—a forty-room castle with seven bathrooms in Saint-Martin-des-Champs, about an hour from the capital, where Fath and his wife Geneviève welcomed hundreds of guests at parties and masked balls

- Église Saint-Pierre de Chaillot, 31, avenue Marceau (16th)—4,000 people attended the designer's funeral at this church

- Jacques Fath Parfums, 12, avenue Victor Hugo (16th)—this recently revived perfume store is located near the Arc de Triomphe

Hubert de Givenchy (1927-2018)

Givenchy was born to be a designer if anyone was. Even as an eight-year-old, he loved feeling the fabric and examining the design of old costumes in his grandmother's closet. He enjoyed drawing, studying sketches in women's magazines, and seeing the couture houses on occasional trips to the French capital. Life was not always easy for the family after his father died before the boy was three. Still, the affection and sacrifices of his mother plus the presence of a large extended family made for a happy childhood in Beauvais. An event that clenched his desire to enter the world of fashion came at age ten on a visit to the Exposition Universelle des arts et techniques in Paris. Seven years later the teenager was back in the city, doing an apprenticeship with couturier Jacques Fath and studying at the École des Beaux-Arts. Givenchy went on to work at other high fashion houses before opening his own company in 1952. His innovative designs—mixing and matching jackets, blouses, skirts, and trousers—earned him the title "enfant terrible de la couture." Early on in his solo career, he met Audrey Hepburn who used his styles in films such as *Sabrina*, *Charade*, and *Breakfast at Tiffany's*. His list of famous clients is a literal who's who of the time: Bacall, Bergman, Dietrich, Jackie Kennedy, and Grace Kelly, to name a few. In 1995 Givenchy retired to the Château du Jonchet, two hours southeast of Paris, where he lived until his death with his longtime partner, designer Philippe Venet.

Addresses for Givenchy

- 39, avenue Pierre-le-1er-de-Serbie (8th)—in the fall of 1945 he interviewed and got a job as an apprentice with Jacques Fath
- École des Beaux-Arts, 14, rue Bonaparte (6th)—Givenchy studied drawing at this well-known fine arts school
- 21, place Vendôme (1st)—he worked for Elsa Schiaparelli at this address in 1947
- 8, rue Alfred-de-Vigny (from 1952 to 1958) and 3, avenue George-V (both in the 8th)—past and present sites of the Maison Givenchy
- Cimetière de Passy, 2, rue du Commandant Scholesing (16th)—at his death at ninety-one Givenchy was buried in this cemetery

Paul Poiret (1879-1944)

Never prone to modesty Poiret entitled his 1931 autobiography *The King of Fashion*. The irony is that by then his reign as a top designer was a thing of the past. The teenaged Poiret began fashioning styles on a small mannequin at home. After dressmakers and designers bought several drawings, he was hired at nineteen by couturier Jacques Doucet to dress high-society figures like actress Sarah Bernhardt; Poiret's first creation, a red cloak, sold 400 copies. Later at Maison Worth, his modern clothing didn't appeal to the conservative clientele. By 1903 Poiret was out on his own, showcasing an Asian-inspired line, including a kimono coat and harem pants, and encouraging bras over corsets. A master of marketing, he "worked like a demon" to promote his wares. Using flamboyant window displays at his shop and having his wife model his creations at parties in their palatial mansion, he sent women flocking to buy them. Poiret was first in many ways: the first to introduce designer perfumes and cosmetics, to have a fashion photography shoot, to use the runway, and to take models on a "trunk tour" of the capitals of Europe. In 1912 he opened a school of the decorative arts which gave birth to a boutique selling textiles, wallpapers, carpets, furniture, and the like. But his fashions for women, poorly made and outdated, brought an end to the Poiret dynasty in favor of younger designers like Chanel. Once his business closed in 1929, he took several odd jobs, dying a pauper. His legendary inability to adapt prompted journalist Janet Flanner to call anything fixed and unchangeable "genre Poiret."

Addresses for Poiret

- rue des Halles, no number found (1st)—his family moved here when Paul was twelve

- École Massillon, 2 bis, quai des Célestins (4th)—he was an average student at this school

- 5, rue Auber (9th)—Poiret had elaborate window displays at his first, modest shop before moving on to the rue Pasquier (8th, no number)

- 26, avenue d'Antin, now avenue Franklin Delano Roosevelt (8th)—the lavish mansion where he lived and partied from 1909 to 1924

- 109, rue du Faubourg Saint-Honoré (8th)—Poiret's property, which had a door leading from his house, was used for poetry readings, concerts, and as an art gallery where Picasso first showed his cubist painting "Les Demoiselles d'Avignon"

- 39, rue du Colisée (8th)—he set up a laboratory for perfume development a two-minute walk from his house

- 83, rue du Faubourg Saint-Honoré—his decorative arts line Maison Martine was at this address before moving to 1, Rond-Point des Champs-Élysées (both in the 8th)
- Cimetière de Montmartre, 20, avenue Rachel (18th)—Poiret's grave can be found in division 8

Yves Saint-Laurent (1936-2008)

With his trademark horn-rimmed glasses Saint-Laurent looked more like a professor than a jet-setting fashion designer. Born to the affluent Mathieu-Saint-Laurent family in colonial Algeria, he shortened his name in the '60s when the international press had trouble with its spelling. In 1950 the teenager saw a play whose sets and costumes fascinated him. Four years later his design of a cocktail dress won first prize at an international fashion competition. At the suggestion of the director of *Vogue Paris*, Saint-Laurent contacted Christian Dior about working for him. The young man's mundane tasks on that job soon gave way to submitting sketches. Upon Dior's untimely death in 1957, the twenty-one-year-old Saint-Laurent was chosen to take over the reins at Maison Dior—giving birth to his nickname "le Petit Prince de la haute couture." The first collection, which he had a mere two months to prepare, was a triumph. His subsequent time doing military service was marred by bullying from other soldiers. Then, upon learning he was fired from Dior, he fell into a depression—initiating lifelong alcohol and drug abuse. Opening his own fashion house in 1962, Saint-Laurent developed styles which revealed an appreciation of art and exotic designs. By 1966 he femininized tuxedos, pant suits, and trench coats, hoping "to reassure women, to give them confidence." That same year, wanting to dress clients from diverse income levels, he achieved immediate success with his Rive Gauche ready-to-wear line. Just before his death from brain cancer, Saint-Laurent formalized a civil partnership with his longtime lover and business partner Pierre Bergé.

Addresses for Saint-Laurent

- École de la Chambre Syndicale de Couture Parisienne, 119, rue Réaumur (2nd)—in 1955 he spent a few months studying at this fashion school

- 30 bis, rue Spontini and 5, avenue Marceau (both in the 16th)—the location of two of Saint-Laurent's former couture houses. The designer spent thirty years at the second site which now houses a museum devoted to him.

- 21, rue de Tournon (6th)—Catherine Deneuve was in attendance when Saint-Laurent opened his first prêt-à-porter shop at this address on September 26, 1966

- 55, rue de Babylone (17th)—where he lived from 1970 until his death; a commemorative plaque marks the building

- Église Saint-Roch, 296, rue Saint-Honoré (1st)—site of Saint-Laurent's funeral before his burial in Marrakech, Morocco

- Maison Yves Saint-Laurent, 23, rue de l'Université (7th)—current address of the couture house

- 53, avenue Montaigne (8th) and 9, rue de Grenelle (7th)—two Saint-Laurent boutiques are found at these locations

Louis Vuitton (1821-1892)

Ambition and determination to make his way in the world were part and parcel of this man's character. After his mother died when he was ten, the boy found himself at odds with his father's new wife. So, at age thirteen Vuitton decided to leave his home near the Swiss border and walk to Paris nearly 300 miles away. In over two years on the road he took odd jobs to support himself and sought shelter wherever he could. Arriving in the French capital, he apprenticed with a box maker. In a short while, the inventive, hardworking young man became a leader in the field. His skills caught the attention of Napoléon III's wife, Empress Eugénie, who then hired Vuitton to be her personal box maker as well as packer of her clothing for trips. A good gig, for sure, especially since her recommendation led to other royal and upper-class clients. In 1854 Vuitton decided to open his own shop in central Paris with a sign outside that read: "Securely packs the most fragile objects. Specializing in packing fashions." Four years later he developed modern canvas-covered trunks which were waterproof, flat, and stackable. Because of these innovations, his store on the rue Scribe was even more successful than before. At the new address the company began focusing on luxury items, and during the Exposition Universelle in 1889 Vuitton received a gold medal and grand prize for his products. Vuitton's son Georges created the iconic company monogram as a way to honor his father four years after his death.

Addresses for Vuitton

- 4, rue des Capucines, at the time called the rue Neuve des Capucines (2nd)—site of the original Louis Vuitton store in 1854

- 1, rue Scribe (9th)—he moved his business here after his large workshop in Asnières, north of the city, was destroyed during the Franco-Prussian War

- 101, avenue des Champs-Élysées (8th)—the flagship store of Louis Vuitton is located here; Snobs will love it but the prices will come as a shock to Cheapos

Chapter 11

Photographers

SINCE TIME IMMEMORIAL, INVENTORS had been attempting to perfect an apparatus for taking pictures. The early nineteenth century saw real progress in the development of the camera—with Frenchmen Nicéphore Niépce and Louis Daguerre at the forefront. These two pioneers paved the way for other trailblazers in their country like Félix Tournachon (known as Nadar), who, along with a massive number of celebrity portraits, was the first to experiment with shots taken from the air as well as in the dark of the Catacombs. One reaction to the turmoil of the two world wars was French humanist photography. This movement allowed people such as Henri Cartier-Bresson, Robert Doisneau, Janine Niépce, and Willy Ronis, to affirm with their photos the idea of an underlying, kind human nature. In these pages we'll take a look at these important names in the field of photography.

Henri Cartier-Bresson (1908-2004)

This shy photographer, who did portraits of Camus, Colette, and Matisse, didn't like to have his picture taken. Because of his reticence at being photographed, Cartier-Bresson's face is hardly known. He traveled widely in his youth, being the son of a wealthy textile merchant. Preferring art to the family business, he did a year of rigorous study with painter André Lhote—learning "photography without a camera." In 1932 after seeing an inspirational photograph, he bought a Leica to devote himself to the seventh art. Cartier-Bresson covered the chrome parts of his camera with black tape, trying to be as unobtrusive as possible, and never used a flash which he considered impolite. Unless a job required color pictures, he favored using black and white film. From 1936 to '39, believing that cinema had a greater impact, he served as Jean Renoir's assistant—even appearing in front of the camera in a few of the director's films. During World War II Cartier-Bresson was a corporal in the French army and spent nearly three years as a prisoner of war. Once he escaped, he joined the Resistance and took pictures at the Liberation of Paris in 1944. Three years later he helped found Magnum Photos, a photographic cooperative created to "feel the pulse" of the times. Cartier-Bresson was assigned to India and China and received international recognition for, among other things, shots he took of Gandhi's funeral. A master of candid photography, he believed that a photo "could fix eternity in an instant." In his later years, Cartier-Bresson came full circle by returning to drawing.

Addresses for Cartier-Bresson

- 31, rue de Lisbonne (8th)—childhood home of the photographer

- Lycée Condorcet, 8, rue du Havre (9th)—Cartier-Bresson attended this high school

- 18, rue d'Odessa (14th)—in 1927-28 he studied art at the atelier of André Lhote

- Café Cyrano, place Blanche (9th)—he socialized with Surrealists like André Breton at this former café

- 37, rue Neuve-des-Petits-Champs, now rue Danielle Casanova (1st)—in 1937 Cartier-Bresson married his first wife, a Javanese dancer, who lived with him on the fourth floor of this building near the place Vendôme

- 198, rue de Rivoli (1st)—he made his home here overlooking the Tuileries Gardens for many years

- Fondation Cartier-Bresson, 79, rue des Archives (3rd)—this foundation, created in 2003, is a major photographic institution housing rotating exhibits as well as preserving Cartier-Bresson's legacy

Robert Doisneau (1912-1994)

Talk about iconic photos: Eisenstaedt's couple kissing in Times Square on V-J day and this photographer's classic of a couple smooching in front of Paris's city hall. Early on the orphaned Doisneau studied to become a graphic designer in advertising. But once introduced to avant-garde artists, he began experimenting with cameras. Shy, he first aimed his Leica at inanimate objects such as cobblestones before focusing on children and later adults. For five years Doisneau served as staff photographer at the Renault factory in suburban Billancourt but was fired for excessive tardiness. As a freelancer, he worked for the Rapho photographic agency, as well as *Vogue* and *Life* magazines photographing celebrities like Bardot and Picasso. But his true passion was recording the lives of ordinary people on city streets: "I had fun throughout my lifetime, building my own small theater." Doisneau also unearthed his drawing skills during World War II to forge papers for the French Resistance. He received many prizes for photojournalism including France's Grand Prix de la Photographie in 1983. Toward the end of his life, he suffered a controversy associated with his famous kissing photo. When a man and woman falsely claimed they were the people pictured, Doisneau revealed that he had set up a series of shots with another couple on the street. The uproar over the staged photograph, plus the death of his wife, caused him great sorrow. According to his daughter Annette: "it's fair to say he died of sadness." Yet his enduring archive of 450,000 negatives displays his humanity, vitality, and humor.

Addresses for Doisneau

- École Estienne, 18, boulevard Auguste Blanqui (13ᵗʰ)—Doisneau took courses in lithography and engraving at this school from 1925 to 1929

- Chez Fraysse, café once located at 21, rue de Seine and Café de

Flore, still going strong at 172, boulevard Saint-Germain-des-Prés (both in the 6th)—settings of many Doisneau photos, the first also a hangout of his friend, poet Jacques Prévert

- Hôtel de Ville, place de l'Hôtel de Ville (4th)—city hall and site of his kissing photo

- 46, place Jules Ferry in Montrouge—this address, just across the city limits from the 14th arrondissement, was Doisneau's longtime home with his wife and daughters

Nadar [Félix Tournachon] (1820-1910)

A self-defined "real daredevil," Félix Tournachon certainly wasn't afraid to tackle new ideas. Most famous as the pioneer photographer who raised the incipient genre to the level of art, he worked as a journalist, novelist, and caricaturist before picking up the camera. As a young man, he studied medicine in Lyon until the death of his father put a strain on finances. Parisian friends like Baudelaire (using the trend of adding "dar" to the end of names) began calling him "Tournadar" which was eventually shortened to his pseudonym. In 1854 his "Panthéon Nadar" of 249 writers in caricature was printed as two gigantic lithographs. Soon afterwards, building on his growing celebrity, he decided to use portrait photography for a second sequence. A serious artist, Nadar preferred using daylight and natural poses for his photos of the Parisian élite...everyone from Victor Hugo and George Sand to Sarah Bernhardt and Josephine Baker. But Nadar was curious about other new inventions of the time as well. The first to take aerial photographs from hot-air balloons, he also experimented with magnesium powder for lighting to shoot pictures in the dark of the Catacombs and sewers. Besides his photographic work, Nadar had a giant hot-air balloon built to take a dozen passengers aloft at a time, serving them cold chicken and wine...and inspiring Jules Verne's novel *Five Weeks in a Balloon*. During the Siege of Paris from 1870 to '71 Nadar organized the first airmail delivery service by way of balloons. Since 1955 the annual Prix Nadar has been awarded for the best photography book published in France.

Addresses for Nadar

- 195, rue Saint-Honoré (1ˢᵗ)—Tournachon was born here

- Lycée Condorcet, 8, rue du Havre (9ᵗʰ)—he studied at this school then called the Collège Bourbon

- 113, rue Saint-Lazare (8ᵗʰ)—Nadar opened his first atelier in the mid-1850s

- 35, boulevard des Capucines (9ᵗʰ)—from 1860 to 1872 he had a larger studio with a glass roof at this location; in 1874 he lent the space to artist friends for their first Impressionist exhibit

- 51, rue d'Anjou [Saint-Honoré] (8ᵗʰ)—his atelier moved to this address in 1874

- Cimetière du Père Lachaise, 16, rue du Repos (20ᵗʰ)—Nadar's grave is in division 36 of this cemetery

Janine Niépce (1921-2007)

This trailblazing photojournalist documented the daily life of generations of French women. A distant relative of *camera obscura* inventor Nicéphore Niépce, she lost her mother at four and was raised by a father who fostered non-traditional attitudes about women and work. While studying pharmacy at the Sorbonne, Niépce also took courses in art and archeology where she found inspiration in Dutch paintings of people at home. Assigned to take photographs for a class, she bought a German Rolleiflex camera, developing pictures in the family bathroom. After a correspondence course in photography, she was determined to create "some images of our epoch." Reacting against sexist attitudes of the Nazis, Niépce joined the Resistance, developing films of German defensive positions and shooting pictures at the Liberation of Paris. At war's end her position with the French Tourism Commission helped her learn about areas outside the capital. In 1955, like fellow humanist photographers Doisneau and Ronis, she began working for the Rapho photographic agency. Treating her female subjects with respect without idealizing them, Niépce showed the dignity, resourcefulness, and independence of women laboring on the farm, scrubbing laundry in a river, or driving a team pulling a barge on a canal. In the nineteen books of photographs she published during her fifty-year career, she often juxtaposed images to show the changes in the lives of women over the years, while hoping to "incite young women to vigilance" in the struggle for equality. Her candid shots and portraits are considered a major historical and sociological study of the second half of the twentieth century. Niépce received the Légion d'honneur in 1985.

Addresses for Niépce

- L'Institut d'Art et d'Archéologie, 3, rue Michelet (6th)—Niépce held a degree in art and archeology from the Sorbonne

- 19, rue Rousselet (7th)—her atelier was found for a while at this address

- Centre Pompidou, place Georges Pompidou (4th)—in 1983 Niépce had a solo exhibit at this modern art museum

- Espace Electra, 6, rue Récamier (7th)—a retrospective of her work was mounted here in fall 1998

- Hôtel Niépce Paris, 4, rue Niépce (14th)—both this Hilton hotel and its street are named for the photographer

Willy Ronis (1910-2009)

According to this photographer: "The beauty of the ordinary was always the source of my greatest emotions." And this child of Eastern European immigrants was a genius at revealing the loveliness of everyday people and things. His father worked as a portrait photographer in Montmartre; but the son, a would-be musician, discovered a totally different type of photography at exhibits. In 1936 he began working as a freelancer with his Rolleiflex camera. Pictures Ronis took of demonstrating workers were published in the leftist periodical *Regards*, propelling him into the career of photojournalism. After a break from photography during World War II, in 1946 Ronis took a job with the photographic agency Rapho where colleagues viewed him as a master of proportion and framing images. A 1948 shot he took of his nude wife Marie-Anne at a wash basin was compared to post-Impressionist paintings; Ronis was astonished at the enduring success of this image "published constantly around the world." Positions followed with Air France, *Vogue*, and as the first French photographer to work for *Life*…although he was at times incensed at that magazine and Rapho for retouching his work or captions. In the mid-1960s Ronis was invited to take photographs in East Germany, which became an itinerant exposition in 1974. Five years later Ronis received the Grand Prix des Arts et Lettres for photography from the Minister of Culture. A retrospective of his work in 2005-06 at Paris's City Hall attracted over 500,000 people. One of the major post-war photographers, his unposed, poetic shots are light-hearted, compassionate, and full of joie de vivre.

Addresses for Ronis

- Collège-Lycée Jacques-Decour, 12, avenue Trudaine (9th)—Ronis attended this school

- Société Française de Photographie, 71, rue de Richelieu (2nd)—he discovered a photography different from his father's at exhibits here

- 7, passage des Charbonniers (15th)—he lived at this address with his wife and her son Vincent

- Hôpital Tenon, 4, rue de la Chine (20th)—Ronis died at this hospital at the age of ninety-nine

Chapter 12

Politicians and Military

THE INDIVIDUALS INCLUDED HERE are a varied lot. Chronologically, there's Napoléon III, most famous for transforming medieval Paris into the city it is today…not without controversy. Philippe Pétain's status shifted drastically from a bona fide hero in World War I to a traitor collaborating with the Nazis as head of the Vichy Régime a few years later. Representing the military is Captain Alfred Dreyfus whose unjust sentencing and imprisonment for treason tore the country apart. Léon Blum, the first Jewish prime minister of France, led his Front Populaire party to enact labor reforms as well as advancing women's rights. And last but never least we find Charles de Gaulle. Decorated for valor during WWI, "Deux Mètres" (as he was called because of his height) went on to lead the Resistance in WWII before serving as President of the French Republic for ten years. So here alphabetically are five men who made their mark in the history of France.

Léon Blum (1872-1950)

Leader of the Popular Front party, Blum was the first socialist and the first Jewish prime minister of France. His well-to-do parents kept kosher, observed holy days, and had their five sons celebrate bar mitzvah. Léon's brilliant early school record resulted in acceptance at the élite Lycée Henri IV. Hoping to become a great writer, he enrolled in the École Normale Supérieure in 1890 but was expelled after failing first-year exams. Blum fared much better studying law at the Sorbonne, receiving top honors in 1894. Yet even while serving on the highest administrative law court, he did not abandon his literary penchant. In 1914 Blum published a book on Stendhal and articles he wrote for several journals prompted one scholar to describe him as "the most intelligent literary critic of the time." Blum's entry into politics came after a friend convinced him of the injustice done to Captain Dreyfus. Not wanting "to feed anti-Semitic passions" by defending another Jew, he initially worked behind the scenes advising lawyers for Dreyfus and Zola. But after describing the "bad faith of the government and court" in writing, anti-Semitic epithets were directed at him. Years later, in February 1936 Blum was dragged from a car and nearly beaten to death. When the Front Populaire was elected that same year, Blum, as premier, negotiated labor reforms including wage increases, the right to strike, and a forty-hour work week. The new leftist majority also began to advance women's rights. Blum's staunch opposition to the Vichy government in WWII led to his imprisonment in Buchenwald and Dachau but he was ultimately liberated by the Allies.

Addresses for Blum

- 243, rue Saint-Denis (2nd)—Blum was born above his parents' store at this location

- Lycée Charlemagne, 14, rue Charlemagne (4th)—a brilliant student at this school, he was then admitted to the Lycée Henri IV, 23, rue Clovis (5th) in 1888 where he met André Gide

- École Normale Supérieure, 45, rue d'Ulm (5th)—Blum passed the entrance exam for the prestigious school in July 1890 but failed finals the following year

- Grande Synagogue de Paris, 44, rue de la Victoire (9th)—Blum married his first wife here

- 38, rue Guynemer, then called the rue du Luxembourg (6th)—a plaque marks the address where he lived from 1897 to 1908

Alfred Dreyfus (1859-1935)

A scandal that shook France to its core was the Dreyfus Affair. At its center was a captain in the army who had moved with his affluent family to Paris after their native Alsace had become part of Germany in 1870. The young man was quite successful in military school, but rampant anti-Semitism resulted in a general giving him poor marks for "likability," stating blatantly that "Jews were not desired" as officers. In 1894 French intelligence discovered a note indicating that a spy was passing information on artillery parts to the Germans. That October, based solely on the resemblance of Dreyfus's handwriting to the note, the captain was arrested and found guilty of treason. A few months later he was publicly degraded at the École Militaire, the buttons and braid cut from his uniform and his sword broken—while a crowd outside the gates shouted "Death to Judas, death to the Jew." But the story doesn't end with Dreyfus's imprisonment on Devil's Island in French Guiana. After the real spy was found in 1896, the army made an all-out effort to cover up the truth. Author Émile Zola's famous letter *J'accuse* in early 1898 led to a second trial but Dreyfus was again deemed guilty. Public outcry led to his release the following year and in July 1906 he was finally exonerated by a military commission and readmitted into the army. Although he acknowledged being "broken body and soul" by his ordeal, Dreyfus remained a soldier, even serving on the front lines at Chemin des Dames and Verdun during World War I.

Addresses for Dreyfus

- College Sainte-Barbe, once found at 4, rue Valette (5th)—he attended this school to prepare for entrance to the then élite military École Polytechnique

- Grande Synagogue de Paris, 44, rue de la Victoire (9th)—site of the marriage with his wife Lucie

- 24, rue François 1er (8th)—when first married, the couple lived at this address before moving to 6, avenue du Trocadéro (16th)

- École de Guerre, 1, place Joffre (7th)—Dreyfus entered this officer training school in the fall of 1891, graduating ninth in his class

- Prison du Cherche-Midi, 52-54, rue du Cherche-Midi (6th)—after his arrest, Dreyfus was taken to this former military prison

- 5, rue de Logelbach (17th)—in 1926 he, his wife, and mother-in-law lived at this location

- 7, rue des Renaudes (17th)—a white plaque marks his residence from 1928 until his death

- 116-118, boulevard Raspail (6th)—the statue *Hommage au Capitaine Dreyfus* with his broken sword stands in a small park near this address; there is a copy at the Musée d'art et d'histoire du Judaïsme, 71, rue du Temple (3rd)

- Cimetière du Montparnasse, 3, boulevard Edgar Quinet (14th)—Dreyfus and his family are buried in division 28 of this cemetery

Charles de Gaulle (1890-1970)

"Deux Mètres" stood out in any situation—by his height as well as his unyielding nature. From a family steeped in French history, the boy devoured books on the country's past and military strategy. De Gaulle's grades improved decidedly once he chose to attend the Saint-Cyr military academy. His commanding officer at the school wouldn't promote him to sergeant because he felt the arrogant student would "only feel at ease as a general!" WWI, however, proved de Gaulle's mettle: he was wounded, decorated for valor, and taken prisoner at Verdun. In officer training following the conflict, de Gaulle criticized his superiors for continuing trench warfare instead of using tanks and planes. As Pétain prepared to sign the armistice with Germany, de Gaulle fled to England to lead the French Resistance. His BBC radio appeal on June 18, 1940 sent home a message of hope: "France has lost a battle; she has not lost the war." At Liberation in August 1944, de Gaulle had General Leclerc symbolically drive tanks into Paris, feigning the French single-handedly liberating themselves. De Gaulle served as head of the provisional government, later as prime minister, and then president from 1959 to 1969. He dealt with problems like the Algerian War and the student revolt in May '68, but his 5th Republic established more executive power, encouraged economic growth, and developed a "politics of grandeur" for France's status in the world. De Gaulle resigned in 1969 and died a year later. A stern, reserved man, he was nevertheless devoted to his wife and his children, especially daughter Anne who had Down's Syndrome.

Addresses for de Gaulle

- Collège Stanislas, 22, rue Notre-Dame-des-Champs (6th)—De Gaulle attended this prestigious private school

- École de Guerre, 1, place Joffre (7th)—he completed officer training at this section of France's École Militaire

- Hôtel de Matignon, 57, rue de Varenne (7th)—he lived here while serving as prime minister for a few months in 1958

- Palais de l'Élysée, 55, rue du Faubourg Saint-Honoré, (8th)—official residence of the president of France located near the Champs-Élysées where de Gaulle lived for ten years

Napoléon III [Charles-Louis Napoléon Bonaparte] (1808-1873)

"Napoléon le petit," as he was disparagingly called by Victor Hugo, was the nephew of "Napoléon le grand"—whose young son had officially been Napoléon II for twenty days after Waterloo. Forced into exile following the defeat, Louis Napoléon's family escaped to Switzerland where he recalled the adoration heaped on his uncle and received training from his mother in preparation for the eventual return of the dynasty. In September 1848 he got his chance: after three months as a member of the National Assembly, he became the first French president elected through universal male suffrage. On December 2, 1851, with the army's help, he organized a bloody coup-d'état to establish his authoritarian Second Empire, enraging many former supporters. Two years later he married the Parisian-educated

Spanish countess Eugénie who soon gave birth to a male heir. As emperor, Napoléon III waged wars in Russia and Mexico, but also expanded the economy by building new train stations and department stores. Of course, he is especially remembered for reconstructing the city of Paris. Aided by Prefect Haussmann and a large map on the wall of his office, the emperor set about the immense task of adding new arrondissements, an opera house, a hospital, parks, a reservoir and sewers. He decreed that buildings along the newly constructed avenues would be the same height, style, and stone. By the 1860s the emperor's health worsened. In the Franco Prussian War a decade later the French army was defeated and Napoléon III was taken prisoner, ending the Bonaparte rule. He spent his final years in exile in England where he died at age sixty-four.

Addresses for Napoléon III

- 8, rue Cerruti, now 17, rue Laffitte (9th)—Louis Napoléon was born at this address

- 14, rue du Cirque (8th)—he lived here for a while with his mistress Harriet Howard (née Elizabeth-Ann Haryrett), a British actress

- Hôtel du Rhin, 4, place Vendôme (1st)—his residence and head-quarters while running for the National Assembly, symbolically facing his uncle Napoléon Bonaparte's statue atop the column in the center of the square

- Palais de l'Élysée, 55, rue du Faubourg Saint-Honoré, (8th)— Napoléon III lived in the official residence of the leader of France

- Notre-Dame de Paris, 6, parvis Notre-Dame (4th)—after a civil ceremony in the Tuileries, he married Eugénie at this cathedral in January 1853

Philippe Pétain (1856-1951)

From hero to traitor in a matter of years: the "Lion of Verdun" of the First World War turned Nazi collaborator heading the Vichy government in the Second. Schooled as a soldier at Saint-Cyr and in Paris, he was de Gaulle's first colonel and taught the young soldier "the Art of Command." During WWI, Pétain really came into his own as a successful commander on the Western Front. A soldier's soldier, he boosted the morale of his exhausted men by providing more rest, furloughs, and moderate discipline. Pétain triumphed at the crucial battle of Verdun using a continuous stream of artillery, ammunitions, and fresh troops. For his valor, at war's end he was granted the distinction of Maréchal de France and was summoned to the signing of the peace treaty at Versailles. After the German invasion in 1940, the eighty-four-year-old Pétain was appointed deputy prime minister in order to inspire spirit into the French Army. Then, on June 16, he became prime minister, signing the armistice with Germany a mere six days later. In Vichy, his "Free Zone" government was nothing more than a puppet of the Germans. Individual liberties, political parties, and labor unions were abolished. Jews were first banned from civil service, teaching, and media jobs. Mass deportations and massacres followed. At a trial for treason after the war, Pétain was condemned to death but because of his advanced age and early military service, his sentence was narrowly commuted to life imprisonment. He died and is buried on the Île d'Yeu off the western coast of France.

Addresses for Pétain

- École Supérieure de Guerre, 1, place Joffre (7th)—Pétain attended this officer training school once found within the École Militaire

- Hôtel de Ville, place de l'Hôtel de Ville (4th)—in April 1944 the doddering leader gave a speech in front of Paris's city hall

- Palais de Justice, 10, boulevard du Palais (1st)—he had two small rooms at the same location as his trial

Chapter 13

Other Famous Frenchmen

THE INDIVIDUALS IN THIS chapter were honestly just plain difficult to fit in anywhere else, mostly because of their unique careers. But then there's hard-to-classify Jean Cocteau, a man who seemed to have a finger in every pie from writing to art to filmmaking. You'll also meet Louis Blériot, the indefatigable, crash-prone pioneer aviator who made the first flight over the English Channel. Among the others are three scientists who worked in fields which are poles apart. These include the great "father of microbiology" Louis Pasteur, the developer of the prepared childbirth method Fernand Lamaze, and oceanographer Jacques Cousteau. And we'll take a look at the "poet of silence," the world-renowned mime artist Marcel Marceau. Finally, two other men who share this space are the brilliant scholar/ professor turned Nazi sympathizer Bernard Faÿ and Louis Braille, an inventor, who provided blind people like himself with the means to read, write, and learn.

Louis Blériot (1872-1936)

One biographer points out that Blériot was "the most accident-prone pilot who had ever flown." With over fifty crashes to his name, that's probably true. But as a pioneer in the field trying to perfect the first flying machine, this heroic aviator gallantly suffered the inevitable consequences. Growing up near the Belgian border, Blériot dreamed of adventure. After engineering studies in Paris, he made a fortune building the first headlights for cars and other automotive accessories. Intrigued by an early plane with flapping wings he saw at the 1900 Exposition Universelle, he started building his own bird-like "ornithopters." Blériot experimented with a series of gliders towed on the Seine and box-kite planes. When those failed to fly, he turned to monoplanes. By 1907, with six years of development and $150,000 investment behind him, Blériot made his first successful flight in Paris. Shortly following Wilbur Wright's public demonstration in France, a London newspaper proposed a 1,000-pound prize if someone could manage to fly over the English Channel. The mustachioed pilot took off at dawn on July 25, 1909 and successfully made the thirty-seven-minute, twenty-four-mile flight from Calais to Dover although the landing was a bit rough. The excitement over Blériot's triumph brought in a hundred orders that year for his 25-horsepower Blériot XI. In World War I he produced combat aircraft which several countries began using. Though long retired by May 1927, Blériot was present at Le Bourget airport and was the first person Charles Lindbergh asked to meet after the American's ground-breaking transatlantic flight.

Addresses for Blériot

- College Sainte-Barbe, once found at 4, rue Valette (5th)—he attended the oldest school in Paris for one year to prepare for entrance into a Grande École

- École Centrale [des Arts et Manufactures], formerly located at 5, rue de Thorigny (3rd)—Blériot spent three years at this school, now the location of the Musée Picasso

- Maison Baguès, 73, avenue Daumesnil (12th)—after getting his degree in engineering, he worked for this art lighting firm

- 41, rue de Richelieu (1st)—he opened a showroom to display and sell his car headlights and other automotive inventions; Renault became a customer

- 288, boulevard Saint-Germain (7th)— a white plaque indicates that Blériot died in this house on the Left Bank

- Musée des Arts et Métiers, 60, rue Réaumur (3rd)—the plane the aviator used to cross the English Channel is on display at this museum (see Chapter 3)

- Cimetière des Gonards, 19, rue de la Porte du Buc, Versailles—after a funeral with full military honors, Blériot was buried in this cemetery

Louis Braille (1809-1852)

Inscribed on a bilingual plaque at his hometown of Coupvray, east of Paris, are the words: "He opened the doors of knowledge to all those who cannot see." Because of his intelligence, determination, and motivation, Braille was just the man for the job. At three he lost his vision after an accident with an awl caused an infection in one eye before spreading to the other. In 1819 he arrived at the world's first school for the blind, a run-down former Parisian prison where sixty students endured inadequate meals, damp living conditions, and a single restroom. Despite the grim atmosphere, Braille flourished, excelling in all of his classes, especially music. The only books available at the time used letters handsewn on paper which made for slow, frustrating reading. Once Dr. Pignier became director in 1821, the school's physical conditions and activities improved. One speaker Charles Barbier showed the students the dot-based "night writing" system he had created for soldiers to communicate silently in the dark. The army captain had adapted it for use by the blind, but it proved overly complicated. Thirteen-year-old Braille approached Barbier about possible improvements yet was ignored. Basing his work on the sighted alphabet, the teen experimented at first with dots and dashes—later eliminating the dashes. In 1824 Braille showed his creation to Dr. Pignier and five years later published a book about it. The director of a blind school in California noted that the system "bears the stamp of genius." Braille's other inventions included musical notation for the blind and "raphigraphy" which enabled blind and sighted people to correspond. A century following his death from tuberculosis, Braille was honored when his remains were moved to the Panthéon.

Addresses for Braille

- Institut National des Jeunes Aveugles, formerly at 2, rue des Écoles (5th) and since 1843 at 56, boulevard des Invalides (7th)—starting at age ten Braille attended this school where he later taught; a plaque is found at the original location in the 5th arrondissement

- Église Saint-Nicholas-des-Champs, 254, Saint-Martin (3rd)—at twenty-four he became the official organist at this church before going to the Église Saint-Vincent-de Paul at Square Cavaillé-Coll (10th) a few years later

- Collège de France, 11, place Marcelin-Berthelot (5th)—Braille took courses at this school of higher education

- Le Panthéon, place du Panthéon (5th)—in 1952 Braille's remains (except for his hands) were moved to this mausoleum from Coupvray

Jean Cocteau (1889-1963)

Some folks are just plain hard to categorize; Cocteau is a prime example. A poet, playwright, and novelist, he was also a designer, painter, graphic artist, songwriter, critic, and filmmaker. In fact, forty-five years before Disney's *Beauty and the Beast* there was Cocteau's version. But this artistic genius was not always successful. As a student, he failed the final high school exam (*le bac*) twice. Cocteau, sensing his underlying potential, tried to reassure his mother writing "there is beneath my seeming frivolity something great and profound." Perhaps adding to his struggles was the fact that death seemed to surround him from an early age—his father and uncle committed suicide and several friends died young. As a teenager, Cocteau showed a penchant for writing poetry, gaining him notice among the literati. He would ultimately become an active member in literary and artistic circles, making friends as diverse and prominent as Gertrude Stein, Chanel, Piaf, Proust, Chaplin, Satie, and Picasso. Another friend, Russian impresario Sergei Diaghilev, once made a life-changing statement to

Cocteau: "Surprise me"—which led to the author's 1917 scenario *Parade* performed on stage by the Ballets Russes. Cocteau had love affairs with a few women but mostly with highly successful men such as actors Jean Desbordes and later Jean Marais, the star of *Beauty and the Beast*. In 1928 Cocteau entered a clinic to cure himself of an opium addiction; however, he continued using the drug for life. He was awarded membership in both the Académie Française and the Légion d'honneur.

Addresses for Cocteau

- 45, rue La Bruyère (9th)—the family first lived in Paris with Jean's maternal grandparents

- 62, rue Malakoff, now avenue Raymond Poincaré (16th)—he and his mother moved into their own place at this location in 1907 and later to 10, rue d'Anjou (8th)

- Lycée Condorcet, 8, rue du Havre (9th)—eventually expelled from this private high school for absenteeism, he struggled with classes other than drawing, German, and gymnastics

- École Fénelon [Sainte-Marie], 24, rue du Général-Foy (8th)—he spent his fourth year at this private Catholic school

- 66, rue de Caumartin (9th)—at seventeen he read some of his poems at the apartment of theater actor Édouard DeMax

- Théâtre Fémina, once found at 90, avenue des Champs-Élysées (8th)—DeMax organized a poetry reading at this venue for the eighteen-year-old Cocteau

- Hôtel Biron, 79, rue de Varenne (7th)—in 1908 he had his first solo apartment in this building, now the Musée Rodin

- Société française de secours aux blessés militaires, formerly found at 21, rue François 1er (8th)—during World War I Cocteau volunteered at this forerunner of the Red Cross since his fragile health kept him from battle

- Théâtre du Châtelet, 2, rue Édouard Colonne (1st)—his scenario

Parade, staged through the help of Picasso and Satie, was performed by the Ballets Russes at this theater in 1917

- La Cible, 13, rue Bonaparte (6th)—an exhibition of his art appeared at this former gallery in 1920

- 36, rue de Montpensier (1st)—Cocteau got tired of fans knocking at his door at this address and moved to Milly-la-Forêt, south of Paris

- Le Grand Véfour, 17, rue de Beaujolais (1st)—he loved having dinner with friends like Colette at this luxury restaurant very near his Montpensier apartment

Jacques Cousteau (1910-1997)

A scientist, Cousteau once remarked, is "a curious man looking through…the keyhole of nature, trying to know what's going on." In short, a perfect definition of himself. The French naval officer, unable to pursue his dream of becoming a pilot after a serious car accident, turned his sights to the sea. His first experience holding his breath while diving had come as a boy at a summer camp when his family lived in the U.S. After graduating second from the École Navale, he was assigned to Toulon where he learned to use underwater goggles. Later attempts at creating the Aqualung (now known as SCUBA) led to over 500 dives in the Mediterranean. Cousteau, realizing the military potential of the apparatus, worked with the Resistance during WWII for which he was awarded the Légion d'honneur. In 1950 he converted a British minesweeper into his research boat, the *Calypso*, and went on to invent many other devices for oceanographers. The underwater explorer produced hundreds of books and films as well as his decade-long TV show, *The Undersea World of Jacques Cousteau*. But the great man's life was not without tragedy and controversy. His brother, a Nazi collaborator, barely avoided execution after the war. In 1979 his son Philippe perished in a sea plane accident. After the death of his wife Simone in 1990, Cousteau married a woman who nearly tore the family apart. His funeral mass, held at Notre-Dame, was an honor normally accorded to heads of state. On his tombstone in Saint-André-de-Cubzac, his hometown near Bordeaux, are the fitting words "Papa du globe."

Addresses for Cousteau

- Collège Stanislas, 22, rue Notre-Dame-des-Champs (6th)—Cousteau attended this prestigious private school

- Cathédrale Saint-Louis-des-Invalides, 6, boulevard des Invalides (7th)—the church where Cousteau and Simone Melchior, his first wife and business partner, were married in 1937

- Villa Wagram-Saint-Honoré, 233 bis, rue du Faubourg Saint-Honoré, (8th)—the family had an apartment in this cul-de-sac

- Le Relais de Venise, 271, boulevard Pereire (17th)—a Cousteau family favorite restaurant

- Équipe Cousteau, 40, rue des Renaudes (17th)—address of the Cousteau foundation

Bernard Faÿ (1893-1978)

Respected author, historian, university professor, and art patron, the enigmatic Faÿ was also a blindy devoted Pétainist, fierce anti-Freemason, and active Nazi collaborator. A native Parisian, he was born into a large Catholic, royalist family. A severe case of polio—which often kept the boy reading in bed—left him with a limp for the rest of his life. From the age of seven Faÿ was fascinated by American culture, deciding he wanted to study at Harvard—a dream he would someday achieve. Ambitious and talented, the first French professor of American studies at age thirty-nine became the youngest person ever selected to teach at the prestigious Collège de France. Although he was once engaged to a woman, he discovered his homosexuality when he was a Red Cross ambulance driver in WWI. Nearly killed at the battle of Verdun, Faÿ came away with the Croix de Guerre as well as an everlasting admiration for Pétain. In August 1940 he accepted the position offered by the Vichy government to head the Bibliothèque Nationale. In that role he saved France's literary riches while aggressively pursuing and imprisoning "this monstrous parasite"—as he described members of Freemasonry. Faÿ was later arrested at his library office, had his personal effects confiscated, and was sentenced to hard labor for life. Thanks to family and friends such as Alice B. Toklas, Faÿ, dressed as a priest, escaped to Switzerland in 1951. There he taught college-level literature classes until press reports and student protests forced his resignation. Granted amnesty by French president Coty in 1959, Faÿ never expressed remorse for his actions.

Addresses for Faÿ

- Théâtre de la Cigale, 120, boulevard de Rochechouart (18th)—Faÿ attended the soirées of Étienne de Beaumont in 1924-25 where he met Proust, Gide, Cocteau, and Satie among others

- Collège de France, 11, place Marcelin-Berthelot (5th)—he taught at this prominent university at the beginning of WWII

- 27, rue de Fleurus (6th)—Faÿ often visited his close friend Gertrude Stein at her home

- Hôtel de Laigue, 16, rue Saint-Guillaume (7th)—for a while he lived at this mansion

- Bibliothèque Nationale, 58, rue de Richelieu (2nd)—he served as general administrator of the national library from 1940 until his arrest in 1944

- Église Saint Nicolas du Chardonnet, 23 rue des Bernadins (5th)— Faÿ's funeral mass was held at this church

Fernand Lamaze (1891-1957)

If this physician had followed his initial inclination, he would have become a neurologist...and there would be no Lamaze method revolutionizing childbirth. But, fortunately for mothers, he didn't have the funds to continue into the specialty he first wanted. Lamaze spent two years as an infantry doctor in WWI and then married his field nurse. During the birth of their child, he felt helpless hearing his wife's cries of pain. The attending obstetrician talked Lamaze into joining a fulfilling but at the time often considered "backwater profession." Like many doctors, Lamaze realized that fear added to the pain of giving birth; however, there were dangers involved in overmedicating women in labor. After hearing lectures by British and Russian advocates of natural childbirth, he decided to visit the USSR to investigate the so-called "psychoprophylactic method" developed by obstetricians there. The calm, controlled birth he witnessed was enough to convince him of his future path. In 1947 with another doctor and three midwives Lamaze opened a clinic at a hospital for steelworker families and began educating women about breathing and relaxing muscles during labor. There were some initial failures and partial successes before women started registering at the hospital in droves...some even before they were pregnant. Because of the on-going Cold War, certain medical professionals wondered if they should espouse a method from behind the Iron Curtain. Lamaze endured six years of hatred directed toward him and his research. A dogged and complicated man, the doctor didn't give up on his revolutionary ideas which in time have become a worldwide phenomenon.

Addresses for Lamaze

- Institut des sourds et muets, 254, rue Saint-Jacques (5ᵗʰ)—arriving in Paris in 1910, he served as a boarding school teacher for the deaf and mute

- 21, rue du Dragon—apartment rented by Lamaze and his wife; another was located on the rue du Cherche-Midi, no number found (both in the 6ᵗʰ)

- La Maternité des Bluets-Hôtpital Pierre Rouquès, 4, rue Lasson (12ᵗʰ)—steelworker clinic which accepted the teaching and implementation of Dr. Lamaze's method, later adding an annex a short drive away at 94, rue Jean-Pierre Thimbaud (11ᵗʰ)

- Cimetière de Grosrouvre—site of Lamaze's grave about an hour west of Paris

Marcel Marceau (1923-2007)

The "poet of silence" presented his shows to rave audiences worldwide over a sixty-year career. The first inspiration for mime came when he was a five-year-old boy watching the silent films of Charlie Chaplin. His parents, the Mangels of Strasbourg, came from Jewish roots in eastern Europe; their two sons would later change their last name to Marceau. In 1939 hoping to find safety from the Nazis, the family fled Alsace for Limoges; yet a few years later the father was deported and died at Auschwitz. During WWII thanks to a cousin, the teen-aged Marceau was recruited by a Resistance group that provided children from the Maison d'enfants in Sèvres with forged papers and ID cards before shepherding them to safety in Switzerland. Once the war was over Marceau studied the dramatic arts in Paris. By March 1947 he began performing his answer to Chaplin's Little Tramp: Bip the Clown—a white-faced character wearing a striped pullover and a battered, floppy top hat with a red flower. His tragi-comic acts mimicked everyone from sculptors to matadors and included classics like *The Cage* and *Walking Against the Wind*. Virtually unknown in France, in 1949 he founded his Compagnie de Mime which traveled around Europe, followed by tours in the U.S. and Canada. Twenty years later he opened his first mime school at Paris's former Théâtre de la Musique. Funnyman Mel Brooks gave Marceau the only spoken line in his 1976 film *Silent Movie*: "Non!" During a twenty-year friendship, the mime influenced Michael Jackson with his movements and dance steps. For his war efforts Marceau received the Raoul Wallenberg Medal for Humanitarianism in 2001.

Addresses for Marceau

- Théâtre de la Ville, 2, place du Châtelet (4th)—in 1946 Marceau studied mime with actor Étienne Decroux and later performed here with his own company

- Théâtre de Poche, 75, boulevard du Montparnasse (6th)—he first introduced his character Bip on March 22, 1947, Marceau's twenty-fourth birthday

- Théâtre de la Musique, 3 bis, rue Papin (3rd)—in 1969 he opened his first mime school at a theater once found at this location
- Théâtre des Champs-Élysées, 15, avenue Montaigne (8th)—his mime company performed here
- 17, rue René-Boulanger (10th)—from 1978 to 2005 he maintained his École nationale de mimodrame in this building's basement
- Cimetière du Père Lachaise, 16, rue du Repos (20th)—in September 2007, accompanied by music from Mozart and Bach, Marceau was laid to rest in division 21 of this cemetery

Louis Pasteur (1822-1895)

There are few true heroes in life, but here's one for you. Every day, if we're paying attention, we see some form of this scientist's name on milk cartons, cheeses, juice bottles, etc. For good reason. Pasteur started out as a chemist studying crystals, but, as he once put it, "luck favors prepared minds." While teaching at the university in Lille in 1856, he was asked by a distiller to investigate why the alcohol he produced sometimes spoiled. Pasteur had the idea of looking at a drop under a microscope and found an active organism besides yeast. "The father of microbiology," as he would be called, had discovered germs. His work on beer, wine, vinegar, and dairy products led to patenting the term "pasteurization" in 1865. Besides foods, though, Pasteur examined diseases such as cholera, and yellow and puerperal fever— undoubtedly saving millions of lives—and so much more, including vaccines for rabies and anthrax. He was an ethical man, devoted to his family, but could at times be quite rigid and authoritarian in his role as a scientist and as an administrator. Being a chemist and not a doctor, he sometimes felt the need to use haughty and contemptuous words to try to convince physicians of his findings. Highly decorated during his lifetime, Pasteur was elected to the Académie Française in 1882. Six years later he established the Institut Pasteur, one of the world's first independent research organizations. After a national funeral, his body was first interred at Notre-Dame then transferred to his institute at the family's request.

Addresses for Pasteur

- Institution Barbet, 3, impasse des Feuillantines (5th)—Pasteur lived and studied for a short while at this address; a commemorative plaque is on the building

- Lycée Saint-Louis, 44, boulevard Saint-Michel (6th)—at this school he prepared for entrance into the École Normale Supérieure at 45, rue d'Ulm (5th) where he later served as director of scientific studies

- 44-48, rue d'Ulm (5th)—a plaque to honor Pasteur marks his laboratory; here, he and Dr. Émile Roux developed a rabies vaccine in 1885

- Musée Pasteur, 25, rue du Docteur Roux, formerly rue Dutot (15th)—this museum is the site of the apartment Pasteur and his wife occupied for the last seven years of his life and where the couple is buried

Conclusion

VICTOR HUGO ONCE SAID that anyone "who contemplates the depths of Paris is seized with vertigo. Nothing is more fantastic. Nothing is more tragic. Nothing is more sublime." In this guidebook we have witnessed all three of these aspects of the great city. There are examples of the fantastic in some of the unbelievably extravagant hotels and restaurants, attractions like the beautifully ornate Opéra Garnier, and French people who performed at incredibly high levels in their careers as artists, chefs, singers, and the like. The tragic is also quite evident in the case of Captain Dreyfus who was "broken body and soul" by unjust accusations of treason and his imprisonment on Devil's Island. There was also the composer Georges Bizet's unfortunate death at age thirty-six, believing that his opera *Carmen* was "a hopeless flop." And who could forget the catastrophic collaboration on the part of scores of French citizens...Chanel, Pétain, and Faÿ among them... with the occupying Nazis during World War II. On the contrary, during that same conflict the sublime was evident in the inspiring actions of Charles Aznavour and Marcel Marceau who each received the Raoul Wallenberg Award for their selfless courage in saving the lives of many of their compatriots.

So, my wish is for you to experience what Hugo termed the "vertigo" of Paris. This can best be accomplished, of course, by visiting the city—either in person or virtually. My hope is that while reading this guide you've already felt some of the awesome dizziness associated with discovering the City of Light.

Acknowledgments

FIRST AND FOREMOST, I'D like to express gratitude to my proofreader *extraordinaire* Leona Dufour whose work and devotion definitely improved this text. My sister Susie Ritchie deserves my thanks for being a tireless supporter of both of my books. I also appreciate the suggestions of important French people from my cousin Françoise Moser Rouan. And last but certainly not least I want to thank my editors at Open Books, Kelly Huddleston and David Ross, for their help in deciding how to develop the Cheapo Snob series.

Made in the USA
Columbia, SC
04 January 2021

30318401R00114